FEDERATION SQUARE MELBOURNE

Australia Day, 2010. Photo: John Gollings

FEDERATION SQUARE MELBOURNE

THE FIRST TEN YEARS

SEAMUS O'HANLON

MONASH University Publishing

Monash University Publishing
Building 4, Monash University
Clayton, Victoria 3800, Australia
www.publishing.monash.edu

This book is available online at www.publishing.monash.edu/books/fsm-9781921867668

   ISBN: 978-1-921867-66-8 (pbk)

Cover image: Australia Day, 2010. Photo: John Gollings
Images: All uncredited photos courtesy of Fed Square Pty Ltd

Design: Les Thomas

Printed in Australia by Griffin Press an Accredited ISO AS/NZS 14001:2004 Environmental
Management System printer.

Photo: John Gollings

FOREWORD

When I joined the Federation Square team in 2005, the project, its gestation and birth had been one of the most talked about in Melbourne's urban history. There were still a lot of sceptics, despite the early visitation numbers outstripping any pre-project estimates. Since that time though, the shared vision of its midwives has been vindicated. Conceived both as a statement of identity and a bridge from the old city to the new, 'Fed Square' has become part of the dynamic of Melbourne and Victoria and a platform for its myriad individual and collective forms of expression.

I am often asked about the reasons for Fed Square's success to date and, like the precinct itself, the response is multi-faceted. Ideas about a prosperous and vital city, the potential of remarkable design, visions for the public realm in a civil society, the yearning for a city square, location, location, location, the science behind the evolutionary management of great public places and the strengths of our local community and its harmonious and participatory nature, have all contributed to an equation which has generated more than 80 million visits since 2002.

Indicative of the diverse relationships that Federation Square sustains, Monash University is a key community stakeholder, using the Square as a venue for a range of talks and discussions throughout the year. In talking to University staff about their interest in this book, we were keen to understand the local phenomena from an international perspective and to locate the Federation Square story with the story of major cities in the last 50 years. To that end we are grateful to Seamus O'Hanlon and to the University for this independent review and the insights into the impact that Federation Square has had in its short life. By helping us to understand what was happening here in Melbourne in recent times, a picture has been painted of the kind of society we have wanted and the way a usefully managed public asset can add significant value.

In advance of Federation Square's 10th birthday, the reflection provides further incentive to continue to work with our very diverse constituency to ensure it is one of the great public places of the world.

— Kate Brennan, CEO Fed Square Pty Ltd

Photo: Trevor Mε

ACKNOWLEDGEMENTS

A number of people and organisations have been involved in bringing this book to fruition. Kate Brennan and her staff at Fed Square Pty Ltd have been especially generous with their time and insights, and have always insisted that this book be scholarly as well as accessible. Special thanks are due to Kimberley Polkinghorne for help with assembling the images that so enliven the text. A number of administrative staff at Monash dealt with the legal and contractual arrangements that allowed this project to succeed, while colleagues in History read drafts of the manuscript and provided valuable feedback. Nathan Hollier and Les Thomas at Monash University Publishing are responsible for the impressive style of the book. As ever, Tanja Luckins provided both intellectual and personal support, while Patrick was mostly tolerant of a preoccupied father.

Photo: Peter Hyatt

CONTENTS

Photo: John Gollings

INTRODUCTION

On 26 October 2002, Victorian Premier Steve Bracks officially declared Melbourne's new Federation Square open. Originally planned to be open in time to celebrate the centenary of Federation on 1 January 2001, the Square was more than two years overdue, having endured a rather difficult gestation and birth, with complaints about its design and cost getting a good airing in the media and in popular discussion. But while there was a lot of noise and a lot of disquiet about the Square, in the hearts and minds of many Melburnians something else was happening, and slowly but surely, in the early years of the new century, Federation Square came to be the symbol of us. While some critics continued to lambast the Square, ordinary Melburnians soon turned it into their meeting place and came to see it as the new centre of the city and the natural place to come together with their fellow citizens to have fun, watch major social and sporting events, participate in the life of the city, or to join a protest.

Ten years on, many of us find it hard to imagine Melbourne without Federation Square, which along with its neighbour Flinders Street railway station and the hundreds of trams that pass it every day has become one of the symbols of the city, both nationally and internationally. In many ways, Federation Square, with its distinctive architecture, galleries and cultural institutions as well as numerous bars and restaurants, has become 'there', the central landmark and meeting place that every city needs and that Melbourne has sought for generations. Its mix of straight vistas, hidden surprises, internal and external meeting and gathering places, and its public and private spaces have become a symbol of the new, cool, post-industrial Melbourne.

While Federation Square's quirky geometric design and layout represents a break with Melbourne's rigid gridiron layout and rather austere built form, it complements it and adds another layer to the city's urban fabric. It is symbolic of the latest turn in the city's history and fortunes. As urban historians have long argued, cities are 'palimpsests' in which buildings, structures and features from different eras are layered on top of or beside each other. In building the new, the old is not completely lost; rather it is added to, and something new emerges out of the mix. This is especially true of Melbourne, which has spent its entire existence rebuilding and reinventing itself.

While a series of building booms over nearly two centuries have seen the city significantly altered, unlike some other cities that have been totally destroyed by natural or man-made disasters (including inappropriate development), enough buildings from all of Melbourne's major architectural periods have survived and been augmented and added to rather than obliterated. The city we enjoy today is an amalgam of all that is good (and some not so good) of the many eras of Melbourne.

Live music at Fed Square, 2012. Photo: Carbie Warbie

The Light in Winter, 2012. Photo: Julie Renouf

From a tiny outpost 'village' of empire founded in 1835, a gold rush boom town emerged in the 1850s, and by the 1880s had become a bustling metropolis of nearly half a million people, before it all went bust in the 1890s depression. Out of the ashes of that catastrophe rose the temporary national capital and Moderne city of the early twentieth century, and then later the Modernist, manufacturing-focussed suburban city of the postwar years. From the early 1980s onwards, that city has in turn given way to the contemporary globalised, post-industrial 'events' city we know today. While we lost a number of grand buildings and streetscapes, sometimes, as with Federation Square, the new is better than the old. Many of us lament the destruction wrought to Collins Street and the Victorian city in the 1960s and 1970s, but few tears were shed about the demolition of the ugly 1960s-era Modernist Gas and Fuel Buildings and adjoining windswept Princes Plaza that made way for Federation Square.

This book is a history of the first 10 years of Federation Square. It follows in the wake of an earlier one by Norman Day and Andrew May, and numerous reports and studies carried out by public and private organisations and researchers in the years since. But rather than another study of the architecture of the Square or of the history of the site on which it sits, or indeed an evaluation of its commercial or financial success, this history seeks to locate Federation Square within the new role played by city centres in the economy and culture of the globalising world. It tells the story of the Square's somewhat difficult birth, but also how it became 'the place to be' in Melbourne, and suggests reasons for its success. Questions are also asked about the design and management structure of Federation Square, the tensions between its public and private roles, and about just where in the new 'spectacle-oriented' post-industrial city is the line drawn between which spaces are private and which are public.

Reference is made to the work of two New York-based urbanists, sociologist Sharon Zukin and geographer David Harvey. Thirty years ago, Harvey declared the end of the postwar industrial economy in the West and documented its replacement by the newly emerging post-industrial one, in which finance interests and what would later become known as the 'creative class' became the main drivers of economic growth. More recently, Harvey has lamented the almost total surrender of the city to financial speculation and tourism. At about the same time as Harvey declared Fordism dead, Zukin drew attention to the emergence of the importance of arts and culture to former manufacturing cities that rapidly de-industrialised in the 1970s. Her book *Loft Living* documented the colonisation of former industrial spaces in New York's SoHo district by artists and others, while a later book, *The Culture of Cities*, noted the centrality of arts and culture to urban economics in the 1980s and beyond. An outcome of this process has been the increasing tendency of governments to develop 'trophy' buildings, including new and expanded museums and art galleries, theatres and performance spaces, as well as other cultural centres, as they seek to rebadge themselves as tourism destinations. The most famous of these is Bilbao in Spain with its Frank Gehry-designed branch of the Guggenheim Museum, but there are many others. Federation Square is the most obvious recent local example of an iconic 'signature' building, but most major Australian cities have pursued similar developments since at least the late 1960s.

Zukin's most recent book, *Naked City*, is perhaps the most relevant to this study. In it she asks questions about who the renewed, semi-privatised, culturally vibrant city is for. In New York and elsewhere in the United States, many of the new cultural zones, or what she calls sites of 'authenticity', are in effect private–public spaces with governance structures that are about maximising profits for landlords and commercial tenants while strictly controlling the activities of users and visitors. Many of these places are public squares and streets, but they are removed from democratic governance and policing. Some allow public gathering and protest, but this is at the discretion of a reasonably sympathetic and liberal, but ultimately private, management group whose main concern is private profits rather than democratic ideals. Other places have the opposite management structure, and like Zuccotti Park in Lower Downtown Manhattan – site of the 2011 Occupy Wall Street protests – are privately owned but publicly accessible. However, as we saw with the rather brutal removal of the Occupy protestors in November 2011, management there was not so sympathetic to the right to protest and preferred, rightly or wrongly depending on one's point of view, to put the concerns of local business first.

As a private space managed on behalf of the state by a publicly owned company, Federation Square shares some similarities with these American public–private spaces. One of the creative tensions of the site is the need to find a balance between the public's right to the space and the social and commercial imperatives of managing the site. This dilemma is somewhat resolved by the Civic and Cultural Charter under which the Square operates, and which mandates that at all times the needs of the public must come before those of commerce. But that is all to come. Before we embark on that aspect of the Square's story, it is important that we have a bit of context and history. Chapter One covers the story of central Melbourne since the 1970s, and Chapter Two details the process of the emergence of Federation Square in the 1990s.

Before Federation Square. Photo: John Gollings

CHAPTER ONE

REVITALISING MELBOURNE

The development of Federation Square was part of a concerted effort by successive governments over almost 30 years to reinvigorate central Melbourne after the problems that plagued the city in the 1970s and early 1980s. While today the city centre is a vibrant place of business, culture and leisure, this new-found sense of self hides a series of major crises that enveloped the city as the economy turned from a focus on manufacturing in the postwar years to one based on services in the 1980s and beyond. In the late 1970s and the early 1980s, central Melbourne was a bleak place, busy with office workers and shoppers by day, but essentially empty after hours. Few people lived there, apart from a few wealthy eccentrics and the homeless who took nightly shelter in the Salvation Army's Gill Memorial Hostel in La Trobe Street, or the rather run down 'private hotels' that lined Spencer Street near the railway station.

What is now Southbank, adjacent to the current site of Federation Square, was pretty much abandoned, as old factories that were no longer economically viable lay idle and rotting. Bourke Street was another casualty of changing demographics and technology. As population moved to the suburbs in the postwar years, so too did shopping, as first supermarkets and later department stores followed their customers to the 'cream brick frontier' to the north, south, east and west of the city. In a remarkably short period of time from

the mid-1960s until the early 1980s, Melbourne's most iconic shopping strip, Bourke Street went from being lined with multi-storey department stores from below Elizabeth Street to above Russell Street to seeing almost all of its stores either close or merge to become part of the two national chains, Coles Myer and David Jones. Similar closures affected other older shopping strips such as Smith Street in Collingwood and Chapel Street in Prahran.

The central city and the inner suburbs found themselves in trouble in this period as economic and social changes caused a major drop in population, a sharp decline in employment and a development of a sense of crisis as older manufacturing and architectural landmarks disappeared, and whole industries collapsed. In common with cities elsewhere in the world, the 1970s were not kind to Melbourne. In many places across the globe there was a gap between the end of the old industrial and manufacturing era (sometimes called the Fordist era after Henry Ford) and the triumph of the new post-industrial, information (or post-Fordist) one. As unemployment rose in the Western world in the 1970s and 1980s, it was the old inner-city manufacturing regions that suffered the most. In Melbourne, the fear was that the older regions would be abandoned by people and businesses and, as was rapidly happening in the north-east of the United States, end up as 'doughnut cities',

empty at their cores but thriving at the periphery. Detroit, the place where Fordism was born, is perhaps the poster city of all that went wrong when old industries collapsed. There, in what was once a vibrant and growing city, home of not only the motor industry but the 'Motown' sound that grew out of it, the post-Fordist era has been a disaster. A city that was home to more than two million residents in 1950 now has less than 800,000. A city that was once a symbol of American might and industry is now symbol of its economic and cultural decline.

This chapter looks at some of the problems that faced inner Melbourne in the 1970s (and seemed to re-emerge in the major recession of the early 1990s), and some of the attempts to solve these problems implemented by successive governments in the 1980s, 1990s and beyond. Federation Square was one highly visible means of bringing life and vibrancy to the city and state's economic core.

THE CRISIS CITY: MELBOURNE IN THE 1970s

As with many other Western cities, Melbourne in the 1970s was in real trouble. As old manufacturing industries died in the face of competition from newly industrialising countries in Asia and elsewhere, there developed a sense that Melbourne's days of economic and social pre-eminence might be coming to an end. As manufacturing declined in importance, newer industries such as financial services, the media and hi-tech services appeared to be locating in Sydney, then fast becoming Australia's gateway city. There was also population drift to Queensland, which was going through a resources and tourism boom, and to a lesser extent Western Australia, which was experiencing massive investment in resource-based projects. A strong sense emerged that, like many other Western cities, Melbourne was entering a period of decline. This was most noticeable in the central city, which in the wake of the collapse of the property boom in the mid-1970s was pock-marked with numerous 'bomb sites' temporarily in use as car parks. The broader inner-suburban area also began to experience de-industrialisation and economic stagnation from the mid-1970s onwards.

Various government and private reports confirmed this decline. In 1977 Melbourne's then urban planning authority, the Melbourne and Metropolitan Board of Works (MMBW) issued two reports on the city's inner area. The first, a position statement on the current state and future prospects of the region, noted the ongoing decline in blue-collar employment in inner Melbourne and warned of the potential for 'serious problems of chronic unemployment' to develop among unskilled workers and others unless efforts were made to generate alternative employment strategies for people displaced by economic restructuring. The second report, *Socio-economic Implications of Urban Development* by Frank Little of Urban Economic Consultants, also voiced concerns about the effects of economic change on inner Melbourne, but was much more alarmist in tone, declaring that the region was experiencing a 'crisis' in manufacturing that was rapidly leading to de-industrialisation, economic stagnation and rising unemployment. The report suggested that if these trends were left unchecked there was a possibility of the emergence of the sorts of problems of urban decay and social disorder that were increasingly plaguing British and American cities and regions. Drawing on the work of US sociologist Daniel Bell, the Little report suggested as in many cities across the Western world, the industrial era was coming to an end in Melbourne, and that in order to ensure economic success in the 1980s and beyond, planners, politicians and business people should immediately institute policies that would facilitate 'the transfer from an industrial to a post-industrial economy'. 'Trying to put off the change', Little warned, 'will only lead to ultimate collapse of [the manufacturing industry] as its structure becomes increasingly outmoded and uncompetitive'.

As the home of much of Australia's heavily tariff-protected manufacturing industry, Melbourne was particularly vulnerable to economic restructuring and a changing international economic order. The city's problems and its exposure to what became known as 'sunset' industries were further exposed in the recession of the early 1980s, when unemployment climbed to beyond 10 per cent for the first time since the 1930s. Former Labor treasurer Rob Jolly recalls that by the time the Cain government was elected in April 1982 real concerns existed about Melbourne's future prosperity. He remembers the inner city as being in decline, with its economy lacking 'long-term growth opportunities' in new industries beyond its traditional reliance on manufacturing. There was also a sense of physical decay about the place, with the CBD pock-marked by numerous empty buildings and abandoned construction sites that had lain dormant since the collapse of the early 1970s property boom. As Jolly recalls it, whole sections of the inner city, such as the now high-profile Southbank region, were derelict, mostly noticeable for the numbers of abandoned factories and windswept wastelands rather than the workers, residents and fun-seekers we associate with the area today.

Southbank, 1973. Source MMBW Collection. Public Record Office Victoria (PROV)

THE REJUVENATED CITY: MELBOURNE IN THE 1980s

The Cain government's response to the economic malaise facing Melbourne and Victoria more generally was to begin to bring life and 'buzz' back to the inner city. Spectacle, major events and recreation would be used to revive and diversify the urban economy, while at the same time restoring a sense of confidence to the city and its people. Early in its first term, the government explicitly announced a new policy that would see Melbourne's status as a big, diverse and dynamic city become a component of economic policy in the new post-industrial economy of the 1980s and beyond. A 1984 economic development policy document declared that the 'national role of Melbourne as a major trading, cultural and sporting centre' was one of Victoria's competitive economic strengths that could and should be harnessed for economic purposes. Capturing and capitalising on the growing financial importance of professional sport, major cultural events and the increasingly multicultural fabric and creativity of the city would be used as a driver of economic growth. In drawing on these strengths and in seeking to revive the inner city, it was hoped that new industries such as tourism and hospitality and retailing would grow. The glamour of the Melbourne Cup was also to be used to highlight Melbourne's role as the fashion capital of Australia and home of its best shopping.

Tourism and leisure were to become important growth industries across the globe in the 1980s, and the new government was keen to ensure that Melbourne was a player. The first step was to make public resources and expertise available to enhance and, in some cases, build inner-urban sporting and cultural facilities. Along with Planning Minister Evan Walker – a former architect – Treasurer Jolly sought to facilitate economic growth by strategically using government funds to renew what he called the 'physical presence' of the inner city. The idea was to stimulate confidence by bringing a 'sense of vibrancy' to a region that many felt had become dull, unwelcoming and something of an embarrassment. Government money was spent on improving conditions for spectators at major inner-city sporting venues such as the Flemington Racecourse and Olympic Park, the conversion of the former Olympic swimming pool in Flinders Park into the all-weather, multi-use Sports and Entertainment Centre, and the installation of lights at the MCG to allow night matches. Melbourne's popular Friday night football and day–night cricket stem from this period. The government declared the AFL Grand Final 'a major sporting event' and passed legislation to ensure that in future it would always be played at the MCG rather than at the recently completed VFL Park at suburban Waverley. In the largest initiative, the National Tennis Centre was built as both a permanent home for the Australian Open tennis tournament and as a venue for indoor sports and 'associated uses', including rock and other concerts. Completed in time for the 1988 tournament, the centre's retractable roof meant that the tennis could be played under an open sky in January, while at other times it could host major concerts and other indoor events. The centre's eye-catching design was an example of Melbourne's emerging prowess in architecture and structural engineering

Harnessing the tourism potential of the inner city was a key element of the new economic strategy. Along with sport, culture was to play an important role in this process. While recognising that 'prosperity should be based not only on acquisition of goods, but also on participation in a vigorous intellectual, social and cultural life within the community', the new government argued that culture ought to be utilised as a driver of economic development. No doubt driven by concerns that national arts and cultural institutions, as well as funding bodies, were increasingly concentrating in Sydney, the 1984 economic statement noted that 'Melbourne has an unquestioned national

Gas and Fuel Buildings (Federation Square site), 1996. Photo: Ian Harrison, Courtesy State Library Victoria (SLV)

role in Australian artistic and cultural life', but warned that this needed to be underpinned and strengthened in the 1980s and beyond. As with the city's sporting infrastructure, Melbourne's arts and cultural facilities were recognised as competitive economic strengths that could and should become increasingly important components of the urban economy. The State Government undertook to investigate and, where possible, free up centrally located sites potentially suitable for the development of cultural institutions, such as a new museum and State Library. It also promised to make land available cheaply in order to build up new institutions and industries especially in emerging growth sectors such as the media, tourism, leisure and 'creative' industries.

Redevelopment of key inner-city precincts was also a major element of this new economic strategy. Whereas in the United States and United Kingdom, governments had allowed inner-city regions to decline and collapse, the Cain government was determined to revive central Melbourne, mainly because of its symbolic importance to the state's economy as the national and international showpiece and 'front door' to local and international visitors and investors. The redevelopment of the south bank of the Yarra River as a 'southern gateway' to the city and as an arts and tourism zone was a major part of this policy. While urban renewal had begun near there in the 1960s with the construction of the National Gallery and Arts Centre, the Cain government dramatically accelerated the process by taking advantage of the closure of many factories and other sites adjacent to the river to open up the area for comprehensive redevelopment. The nearly complete Victorian Arts Centre was seen by the government 'both as a cultural and economic resource' and as the first stage of a plan to redevelop the Southbank area 'as a tourism and cultural precinct'. Southbank was declared an urban action area and in 1986 a development strategy was launched that sought to re-create the region as an arts, tourism, housing and commercial hub, with these facilities acting as major drawcards for local, national and international tourists. Twenty-five years later, that vision has largely been realised.

While new buildings, structures and sporting and cultural precincts were important, there was also a recognition that a revitalised city needed a vibrant cultural agenda. The Labor government's 1984 economic initiatives statement undertook to begin a campaign to promote Melbourne as a place where things happened. Central to this was an 'events' strategy that would enliven the street, bring confidence to locals, and help in bringing tourists to the city and the inner suburbs. Early in its term, the government sought to emulate Adelaide's success in marketing itself as a 'Festival City'. Existing ethnic and other festivals were funded and expanded, while new ones including Spoleto (later the Melbourne International Arts Festival) and its associated Fringe and Writers Festival were first staged in 1986. The Comedy Festival followed in 1987. As with sporting events, it was no accident that all of these festivals were primarily located in the inner city. This of course partly reflects where the artists live, but it was also part of the deliberate policy to enliven the streets and neighbourhoods of the inner city. For a time it all seemed to work and in the late 1980s the central city seemed to be on its way back. During the state election campaign of 1988 Premier Cain was to boast of the number of cranes on Melbourne's skyline as a surge of new office and other buildings changed the face of Collins, Bourke and Swanston Streets.

AGENDA 21: MELBOURNE IN THE 1990s

The late 1980s boom came to a shuddering halt early in the new decade. A failed bid to host the 1996 Olympic Games coincided with high-profile public transport strikes and the collapse of a number of Victorian-based financial institutions to sap the life out of local confidence and the city and state economy. The election of the Kennett Liberal government in a landslide in September 1992 was, however, to bring a dramatic turnaround in confidence and a sharp increase in the role of events and culture in Melbourne's economy. The new government's Agenda 21 policy had as its centrepiece the building of new or restored sporting, cultural and entertainment venues that would reinvigorate the central city. Premier Jeff Kennett presented the Agenda 21 policy as a long overdue rejuvenation of the state's cultural assets, but he now concedes it was also a means of bringing life back to the recession-ravaged inner city, and a way of restoring the confidence of a people hurt by the radical restructuring of the economy his government deemed necessary if Melbourne was to prosper into the twenty-first century. Agenda 21 projects were to be the dividend that economic restructuring would pay for. Officially his Minister for Major Projects Mark Birrell presented it as a policy 'committed to rebuilding the city through a schedule of projects to enhance Melbourne's appearance and strengthen its key financial and commercial activities'. Three years later, in an *Agenda 21 Quarterly* issued by his office, Birrell was to claim that since the initiation of the program 'the outward face of Melbourne has undergone a remarkable transformation. New life has been breathed into our city so that it has a sense of purpose and activity not seen for decades.'

While this statement was a deliberate attempt to ignore and downplay the policies and successes of the previous Labor government in Southbank and

Princes Plaza (Federation Square site), 1996. Photo: Ian Harrison, Courtesy SLV

elsewhere, it is true that the mid-to-late 1990s saw a flowering of new projects in central Melbourne. In outlining Agenda 21 in August 1993, Birrell stated that it had four main goals: enhancing Melbourne's attractiveness as a lively cosmopolitan centre with a vibrant retail, entertainment and cultural focus; strengthening the city's key financial and commercial activities; expanding the capital city as a base for trade, advanced manufacturing and research; and promoting Melbourne as a showcase of world-class events and festivals, as the home of the arts, sports and conventions within Australia and within the Asia-Pacific region. Funded in part by revenue generated by the sale of the state's first casino licence, Agenda 21 projects included the building of the Exhibition Centre (dubbed 'Jeff's Shed') on Southbank, the refurbishment

of the State Library and the National Gallery of Victoria, the construction of the new Melbourne Museum in Carlton, the expansion of the National Tennis Centre (and its renaming as 'Melbourne Park') and the construction of Melbourne Sports and Aquatic Centre at Albert Park. The cultural and sporting calendar was also beefed up, starting with the enticement of the annual Grand Prix from Adelaide in 1996, a bid for the Commonwealth Games in 2006, and bids for a number of smaller, but internationally focussed sporting and other events.

The Agenda 21 projects combined with policies and initiatives by the City of Melbourne to rejuvenate the central city. This included bringing back residents through the 'Postcode 3000' policy, which sought to encourage residents to

Demolition of the Gas and Fuel Buildings, 1996. Photo: Ian Harrison, Courtesy SLV

take up abode in empty office and warehouse buildings in the CBD. Together these policies gave Melbourne a new spark, a new sense of life and of itself. The contrast between the faltering city of the late 1970s and the recession-shocked one of the early 1990s, and the lively, vibrant place of the late 1990s and beyond was profound. Statistics on residents, jobs and visitors bear out these changes. In 1991, the population of the CBD and the residential portions of the City of Melbourne was about 34,500, most of whom lived in the designated residential zones of North, West and East Melbourne, Carlton and South Yarra. Fewer than 5,000 lived in the CBD proper. By 2001, this municipal population had grown to more than 50,000, even after boundary changes had chopped some formerly residential areas such as North Carlton and Kensington from the City

of Melbourne. The biggest change was that by the turn of the century many thousands of people were residents of the CBD. Ten years later in 2011, the total population of the by now slightly enlarged City of Melbourne had climbed to more than 96,500 and included sizeable populations in the formerly resident-free zones of Southbank and Docklands as well as the still growing CBD, which overtook Carlton as the largest 'suburb' in the City of Melbourne area in 2002. By 2009, almost 18,000 people lived in the CBD. The population of the inner suburbs also increased dramatically in the 1990s and 2000s. From a postwar low of just over 230,000 in 1986 the population of inner Melbourne (basically the area within a 5 kilometre radius of the CBD) has increased by 100,000 to 330,000 today.

Left: Australia Day fireworks, 2006. Photo: David Simmonds   Above: VOLUME. The Light in Winter, 2009. Photo: Julie Renouf

Most of these extra people are locals, but many are international students studying at public and private colleges, universities and other educational institutions, which have become key employment and activity nodes in the inner city. In 2009, almost 22,000 international students lived in the City of Melbourne, with many thousands more resident in surrounding municipalities. These international students are an integral feature of the vitality of the new Melbourne and are a group that simply did not exist in the early 1980s, when most of the city's student population were relatively poor locals living in share houses in Carlton and Fitzroy. In addition to the new residents, more than a million international tourists visit the city centre each year, while many millions more come from interstate and outside the metropolitan area. As of 2010, an average of 788,000 people per day visit the city centre for business or pleasure.

While tourists and residents are important to the revitalised city centre, so too are jobs. From a low of 277,000 jobs in the recessionary mid-1980s, worker numbers in the City of Melbourne have rebounded to the current figure of more than 400,000. Until the 1970s, a large number of those were in blue-collar occupations such as engineering, warehousing, printing and manufacturing, but today there are almost none of these industries left in the inner city area. Most jobs today are in white-collar industries such as finance, business and administration. Many of these are high-paying professional jobs, but thousands of other people work in the lower-paying end of the economy in the cafes, restaurants, bars, clubs, shops and galleries that serve these people. Today professionals account for more than 40 per cent of all city employees, while what are increasingly called the 'creative class' make up a further sizeable portion.

After suffering significant population and employment decline in the 1970s and early 1990s, inner Melbourne is now one of the fastest growing residential districts in Australia, and has seen significant job growth, especially in the high-paying professional and business services fields. In the 40 years since the 1970s, the inner city has gone from being a place of abandonment and decay to a vibrant region of high-paid jobs, commodified leisure activity and urban spectacle. It is in the context of these changes that we should understand the coming of Federation Square and its place in the 'new' Melbourne. Chapter Two tells the story of the emergence of the idea of the Square and the processes that led to its somewhat difficult birth.

Federation Square riverside. Photo: David Simmonds

The ACMI shell during constructi

CHAPTER TWO
MAKING FEDERATION SQUARE

As Andrew May notes in his 2003 history of the Federation Square site, plans to roof and re-use the air space above the railway lines and yards at Princes Bridge have a long and ignoble history. In the twentieth century alone these ranged from the traditional, in the form of a 1925 plan to create a Cathedral Square providing an open space and vista to St Paul's opposite, through to the award-winning high Modernist Princes Plaza development of 1967, and on to some truly bizarre suggestions arising from the 1979 'Landmark Competition'. Responding to a State Government brief to create an urban landmark to put Melbourne on the world map, architects, designers and amateurs from across the globe put forward proposals that included parks, hanging gardens, civic squares, a big 'M', and a few ideas that were simply weird. Needless to say, no overall winner was chosen, but the perception that Melbourne needed such a landmark showed the depth of despair about the city's woes at that time, perhaps most starkly in contrast with Sydney whose new Opera House had become an instant international icon after its opening in 1973. In the 1980s, the Cain government again kick-started the proposal to open up the area by relocating some railway functions away from Jolimont to outer suburban locations. But other than some land near the MCG that was later redeveloped for residential purposes very little was to come of this process. A 1985 proposal by up-and-coming architectural firm Denton Corker Marshall (DCM) sought to demolish one of the Princes Plaza buildings and build another further east in order to reopen the Cathedral vista, but like so many other proposals this came to nought.

The election of the Kennett government, with its 'can-do' attitude and commitment to major projects, saw change very much in the air. As part of a policy to restart the Victorian economy battered by recession and economic restructuring, the government teamed up with staff at the City of Melbourne to find ways to revive the central city as a place of business and pleasure. The plan was to create a new 'capital city policy' that would reinvigorate Melbourne's infrastructure and thus its 'face to the world'. One element of this was a draft proposal from senior staff at the City of Melbourne to develop what was called 'the Centenary Centre: Gateway to the Melbourne Experience' at the Princes Plaza site, which, drawing on a current and very successful tourism campaign, was presented as the 'access point to every piece of Victoria'. Essentially a garden-based square over the railway tracks, the Centenary Centre was integral to the thinking behind what became Federation Square and was highly influential in the development of what became known as Creating Prosperity – Victoria's Capital City policy, released in November 1994.

Assembling the Labyrinth.

Launched by Kennett as Premier and Minister for the Arts, Creating Prosperity had as its stated aims the need 'to strengthen the economic viability, vitality and image of the central city' and to ensure that it was 'exciting and welcoming to all people'. Under this proposal, the central city – loosely defined as the CBD and its immediate surrounds – was to regain its role as 'the driving force behind Melbourne's intellectual, cultural, retailing, manufacturing and sporting leadership in Australia'. Further, an enhanced and vibrant central city area would maintain Melbourne's focus as a place 'for international investment, business, higher education, research networking, conventions, exhibitions and diplomatic and cultural exchange' as well as an exporter of services in the fields of business, the professions, education, research, communications, advanced manufacturing, health, arts and urban services, particularly to the Asia-Pacific region. The policy also sought to reinvigorate central Melbourne as 'a stage for world-class cultural and sporting events [and] a popular destination for overseas and interstate visitors'. Along with the abandoned old Carlton and United Brewery site at the northern end of Swanston Street, the disused Docklands area to the west and the Jolimont railway yards to the east, Creating Prosperity deemed what was to become Federation Square a 'key site' that could and would be redeveloped in order to create the 'new' Melbourne. The term 'Federation Square' rather than 'Centenary Centre', was used for the first time in this policy, and rather than the redeveloped space envisaged as a passive recreation garden square it would become Melbourne's 'foremost civic site' that would 'unite the city structurally, providing it with a new outlook and symbolising the city's new place in the nation and the world at large'.

Federation Square was to be teamed with a new riverside public park – to be jointly developed by the Victorian Government and the City of Melbourne – which would connect the Square to the sports precinct further east. But while the Square was to be an 'active' place, what was to become Birrarung Marr was more passive, closer perhaps to the original Centenary Centre model than Federation Square. But the story of Birrarung Marr is for another place and another author. Instead this chapter tells the story of the years between the announcement of the vision for Federation Square in November 1994 and its opening in October 2002. It is a story of competitions, controversy, changes of plans and governments, delays and cost overruns, but ultimately of the successful creation of a new public space on a site that had been an eyesore for more than 100 years.

THE COMPETITION

The concept of Federation Square was formally announced in 1996 as a joint venture between the Victorian Government, the Commonwealth Government and the City of Melbourne. In the same year, a preliminary design brief and call for proposals, which invited ideas for the design of the Square from architects and design firms from around the world, was released. This document set out the parameters of the project, the size of the site and its location, as well as the intended uses of the various buildings and spaces. Details of other major projects planned or already underway in central Melbourne were included with Federation Square and highlighted as key to plans to revitalise the city centre. 'Intended to become the central focal point of the city', Federation Square was presented as 'perhaps the most important civic development to be undertaken in the city for many decades. Quality of design is therefore of paramount importance.' Seven 'key objectives' for the project were included in the design brief, including the need for the site to have a social objective and be 'people friendly'; to look ahead culturally and technologically; to meet an identified need for Melbourne to have a new civic and cultural space; to celebrate the city's Indigenous and multicultural heritage and history; to be

Left: Building the deck.

Above: Crossbars and deck sheer stud formation.

architecturally bold, while providing a physical link between the Yarra River and the CBD; and to be operationally and financially sustainable.

Federation Square was envisaged as a 'year-round people place where landscaped indoor and outdoor spaces support festivals, concerts and art exhibitions as well as showcasing the city's screen industry capacity'. In part modelled on nineteenth century European 'wintergardens' and thus usable in a range of weather conditions, the Square was, however, to offer an up-to-date version of this idea by 'integrating nature, creativity, and 21st century technology in a range of enclosed, semi-enclosed and adjoining open spaces'. Four key components were mandated: a civic square of at least 7,000 square metres, atrium and courtyard spaces animated by botanical displays and gardens complemented by food and beverage outlets, secure ('ticketable') performance and exhibition facilities, and a screen culture (Cinemedia) centre. More prosaically, car parking for at least 500 cars was a compulsory element of the project.

From there things became much more lyrical:

Federation Square will be warm and welcoming, stimulating all the senses – the smell of good coffee, the strains of a Mozart string quartet in a comfortable environment, the beauty of a circus artist flying through the roof space, the taste of delicious food and the subtle textures and scents of a range of plants. It is a place where one can meet with friends or be happily alone. It is a place where one can be excited by the technology displays in Cinemedia's discovery gallery or calmed by the experience of spending time in a garden environment.

It has intimate, interesting spaces that one can happen upon and also areas where larger numbers can come together to share the experience of a public occasion both indoors and out. This may take the form of an opening of a festival, a performance of multimedia and live performance or more grand ceremonies of state such as Anzac Day and Australia Day.

February, 2000

September, 2000.

Federation Square, particularly the internal and external garden areas, is safe and comfortable to be in, stimulates the imagination and lifts the spirits whether one visits it alone or as part of a group.

These words and descriptions were certainly evocative and expressive. But the guidelines were also quite prescriptive, with a mandate that the buildings be predominantly low-rise, have active street frontages with multiple faces to the street, and 'acknowledge Swanston Street as the primary ceremonial route of the city'. Outdoor civic spaces were accordingly to be oriented towards Swanston Street and St Kilda Road. The budget was very tight, with all of this (including decking the railwaylines) to cost no more than $128 million, half of which would come from the City of Melbourne and the rest from the Victorian and Commonwealth governments. Perhaps the most popular aspect of the announcement at that time was not the Square, but that as part of the project the hated Princes Plaza and Gas and Fuel Buildings would be demolished. This was a separate budget item, paid for by the Victorian Government.

More than 177 entries were received from around the world, 41 of which came from outside Australia. The United Kingdom provided the largest number of overseas-based entries with 18, while six came from the United States. The selection panel of seven was chaired by Professor Neville Quarry of the University of Sydney, with American-based 'celebrity' architect Daniel Libeskind as an international adviser. Five entries were shortlisted, including those by local firms Ashton, Raggatt, McDougall (ARM) and Denton, Corker, Marshall (DCM), who by the late 1990s were becoming the de facto Agenda 21 architects, having been responsible for many of the other major projects undertaken by the Kennett government, including the Exhibition Centre, the Melbourne Museum and much of the design work associated with the CityLink tollroad project. Another shortlisted entry was by an international firm (albeit one with an Australian-born principal) Lab Architecture Studio of London, which later joined forces with the local firm Bates Smart to refine their design. This entry was unanimously judged the winner in July 1997.

Above: Riverside view. Photo: David Simmonds

Left: The Ian Potter Centre: NGV Australia during construction.

Their winning design was described by the chair of the judging panel Neville Quarry as 'an exciting, original and clever complex of buildings and spaces, which will enrich the city, engage the public with witty and sympathetic architecture and provide an inspiration to Melbourne's heritage'. Premier Jeff Kennett was privately critical, but then and now publicly very supportive of the design, describing it as exhibiting 'boldness, freedom, invention and excitement', while the winning architects said their proposal would 'link Melbourne's past and its future' and was 'futuristic because Melbourne is a futuristic city'.

Others were not so sure. Nigel Flanagan of the University of Melbourne Architecture School thought the designers had 'got it wrong'. His colleague Miles Lewis complimented the proposal as 'a successful and imaginative design' but foreshadowed a future controversy when he expressed concerns that a key feature, the two 'shards' that jutted into the sky over the St Paul's Forecourt would block views of the cathedral to the north of the Square. In later years he would go on to become a major critic of the Square, labelling it as being 'totally out of keeping with Melbourne' and looking like 'somebody's luggage left there and then run over by a car'. Expatriate comedian and professional curmudgeon Barry Humphries labelled the design 'ghastly' and predicted that the futuristic design would quickly date. Years later Miles Lewis was to agree with this assessment prophesying that before long Federation Square would become 'something of an embarrassment' to Melbourne.

The original plan located the two key cultural sites, the Australian Centre for the Moving Image (ACMI) and Cinemedia, at the back of the Square alongside cinemas and broadcast studios associated with multicultural television and radio broadcaster SBS. The performance venue and exhibition galleries were on the northern Flinders Street frontage while a 'desert greenhouse' and a 'riverfront greenhouse' overlooked the Yarra to the south of the site. A long atrium crossed the site from south to north with the Wintergarden forming a hub in the middle. The Wintergarden also acted as a crossover space between the large civic square at the front of the site and the cinematic buildings at the rear. A pub and restaurant faced St Kilda Road near the river, while what was to become the Square's most important and famous feature, the Big Screen, backed onto this building facing the Civic Plaza. Bars, cafes and restaurants faced the Square and were scattered throughout the buildings. The controversial shards faced St Paul's Cathedral in what was known as the St Paul's Forecourt, with the eastern shard planned to host a Federation exhibition and a viewing gallery.

BUILDING AND OPENING THE SQUARE

While the principals of Lab Architecture Studio, Don Bates and Peter Davidson, had extensive experience in teaching and writing about architecture and consulting on issues associated with major projects across Europe, they had no experience in bringing a major project such as Federation Square to fruition. Their link with the long-established Melbourne-based Bates Smart was therefore a key element in ensuring the successful outcome of the project. Lab established an office in Melbourne, and in mid-1998 the construction group Multiplex began work on Federation Square, with completion due in mid-2000 in time to host the celebrations for the centenary of Federation on 1 January 2001. However, a number of alterations to the design of the Square and unforeseen cost increases meant that the already tight time line and budget was never entirely realistic. These changes saw ACMI and its associated facilities moved to the Flinders Street frontage, while the addition of a major new gallery, which became The Ian Potter Centre: NGV Australia (announced during the bidding process), saw the exhibition space expanded and moved to the back of the site. The 'performance venue' (now BMW Edge) replaced the

Construction of The Ian Potter Centre: NGV Australia. Photo: Bonacci Group

As seen from the corner of Russell Street at Night. Photo: Oliver Sperlich

rivergarden and desert garden overlooking the Yarra River, while the shards – especially the western one – were dramatically reconfigured.

These changes were in part responsible for the delay and the extra cost, but in reality the original time line and price tag were always highly optimistic. The construction process was mired in controversies over the design and technical difficulties in achieving the architects' vision at a price that was acceptable to the government. The most publicised difficulty was the western shard, which became the symbol of all that was wrong with a project that by the late 1990s was increasingly being regarded as an expensive exercise in architectural and governmental megalomania. Echoing concerns raised by architectural historian Miles Lewis on the day the winning design was announced, a number of people and groups began to lobby to alter the proposal in order that the height of this shard and its impact on the sightlines from St Kilda Road towards St Paul's Cathedral be addressed. Heritage bodies, most notably the

National Trust, as well as some Melbourne City councillors and the then ALP state opposition, were especially concerned about this and mounted a vigorous campaign to have the shard removed or lowered. In 1998, the final design of the Square saw both shards reduced in height by 2 metres. But this was not enough to satisfy the critics, and when the ALP was elected to government in October 1999, a review by the former planning minister and architect (and 'mastermind' of Southbank) Evan Walker, saw the western shard shrunk to become the two-storey 'stump' that today houses the Melbourne Visitor Centre. Whether this was a good thing is still controversial. The architects openly disagreed with the decision and made their concerns known, while former Premier Kennett has recently called it a 'stupid political decision' that was costly and 'interfered with the architects' grand plan'.

Another factor that led to increasing costs and delays in completion was the structural foundation of the Square, the deck that covers the railway lines

Construction of the deck. Photos: Hyder Consulting

Nearamnew. Photo: Trevor Mein

below, which proved to be an expensive and delicate exercise in engineering. The major problem was vibration from the hundreds of trains that pass below the site every day. In a typical development this would not be a serious problem, as the impact would be absorbed by the walls of the building, but in a structure where the major tenants were cinemas, museums, and a gallery full of art worth hundreds of millions of dollars, vibration was a potentially fatal flaw. Construction of the deck also had to take place with minimal disruption to normal train services. Most of the work was thus carried out between midnight and six in the morning, at overtime rates. In the end, the vibration problem was resolved by sitting the Square on top of more than 4,000 springs, which absorb the impact of the trains. Heavy concrete walls also protect against potential damage from train derailments. As the Square took shape, day-to-day construction was also delayed as the architects and engineers sought to resolve technical questions about how to make the vision become a reality.

Another major undertaking was 'Nearamnew', the elaborate sculptural story told in the Kimberley stone of the Plaza, which was created by artist and writer Paul Carter in collaboration with the architects. Devised while he was writer-in-residence at the Square in 1998, 'Nearamnew' was conceived according to Carter as a 'performative analogue of federalism'. It consists of three parts: a whorl pattern that 'forms the envelope of the design', within which are nestled nine ground figures and visions that underline the sense that this is a site with many stories and meanings for both the Indigenous and non-Indigenous people of what is now Melbourne. Sourcing the stone and laying it added to the cost and time needed to complete the Square. Later, design and construction issues, especially associated with the Atrium and the inclusion of a function centre, were blamed for further delays and cost blowouts. In 2002, the Auditor-General costed these at $42.9 million and drew attention to cost increases associated with what was delicately called

Top: The BMW Edge. Photo: James Braund

Right: Taxi Dining Room.

Left: Interior of The Ian Potter Centre:

NGV Australia. Photo: Ian McKenzie

'the construction of certain structures on the Square'. By May 2003, when most of the Square had been opened to the public, the Auditor-General reported that costs had increased by a further $21.8 million over the February 2002 estimate, the bulk of which was related to building works associated with The Ian Potter Centre: NGV Australia, ACMI and the Plaza.

Whatever the concerns about shards, delays and cost increases throughout the construction process, there was mounting evidence for the inaugural Board chaired by Peter Seamer and stakeholders that Federation Square was a source of curiosity to the public. While many expressed reservations about the unusual design, there was evidence that some at least were positive about the project. A public open day that included tours of the site in November 2000 drew upwards of 15,000 visitors to the site, while another in May 2001 saw more than 20,000 people take advantage of what was described as their last chance to see it before its official opening, by then due in late 2001. Newly appointed CEO Peter Seamer, who took over leadership of the then struggling project in January 2000, recalls the numbers on both days as being closer to 100,000 and sees the November 2000 event as the day when Melburnians took 'ownership' of the Square. As the person in charge of what many people thought of as a folly and a 'white elephant', these open days and the general enthusiasm of the crowds who visited were tantalising evidence that a change in public attitudes might just be in the air. But there was still a way to go.

More than a year later, when Federation Square was finally opened to the public on 26 October 2002, the *Age* reported that Premier Steve Bracks 'spoke enthusiastically to the crowd of about 2,000 people' about 'a striking monument to our Federation ... as complex and intricate as the people who make up our nation'. An invitation-only event the night before had seen 2,000 people cram the Atrium for a black-tie event that, according to Peter Seamer, was only legal because the certificate of occupancy and thus safety was delivered by hand to

The Atrium. Photo: Ian McKenzie

ACMI. Photo: Mark Farrelly

the site manager as the guests began to arrive. Even then, only about two-thirds of the public areas were complete. The two major drawcards, ACMI and The Ian Potter Centre: NGV Australia, were partly opened to coincide with the Square's public launch, but upper-level galleries at the Potter and ACMI's cinemas only came on stream in late November. Restaurants, bars and function centres were progressively opened throughout early 2003. While the opening of Federation Square got the thumbs up from some, others were still to be convinced of the worth of this expensive piece of public infrastructure. The *Sunday Age* reported the opinions of six opening day visitors, five of whom were broadly enthusiastic, while the sixth, a teacher from Edithvale in Melbourne's southern suburbs, saw in Federation Square many of the problems that he felt plagued society more generally.

I think it's very ugly but it reflects a society that has lost the plot as far as aesthetic beauty is concerned. Just imagine what the materials they've used are going to look like in 10, 15 years. It will be even worse than it is now. I've got nothing against modern art or architecture when it's done properly. It's a matter of aesthetics and using your eyes and your senses and using some discrimination.

So, more than eight years and more than $450 million on from the initial announcement of Federation Square in 1994, there were still many people who were unhappy with it. Ten years later, there are still some who see it as a blot on the landscape, and one of the ugliest buildings in the world.

But equally, evidence quickly emerged that many locals were taking to Federation Square and recognising it as the city's new 'civic heart'. Nationally,

NGV Foyer, 2002. Photo: Trevor Mein

Australia Day, 2006. Photo: David Simmonds

and internationally too, it began to make a mark by winning a number of engineering, architectural and civic awards. In 2003, the Square won an Australian Engineering Excellence Award and The Ian Potter Centre: NGV Australia won the Royal Australian Institute of Architects award for interior architecture. A year later, the gallery won the Interior Design Excellence and Innovation Award from the Interior Design Institute of Australia, and in 2005 the International Urban Land Institute of Australia recognised the Square with its Public Project – Award for Excellence for the Asia-Pacific Region. Twelve months later, Federation Square won the Best New Global Design Award in the Chicago Athenaeum International Architecture Award, and local awards from Tourism Victoria and the Victorian Multicultural Commission. In 2008 the Square entered the Victorian Tourism Hall of Fame as a major tourism attraction of Victoria.

Thus perceptions of Federation Square were changing. It was no longer seen as a white elephant, at least by the architectural cognoscenti, and soon after its opening the Square was beginning to work as a space and as a concept. But as discussed in Chapter Three, getting the buildings up and winning design awards was one thing; making sure Fed Square was popular with the people was another. The solution involved finding the right balance between commercial imperatives and community function, and it was this that was central to the success of the Square in its first few years of operation.

Inside the BMW Edge. Photo: Andrew Hobbs

AFL Grand Final, 2009. Photo: Julie Re

CHAPTER THREE

MAKING IT WORK

The need to ensure the financial stability of Federation Square while maintaining and enhancing its function as a community and civic space has been a key driver of design and management from the outset. Thus the design parameters were both lyrical and prosaic. The 'smell of good coffee' required space for customers to park their cars, while the Civic Plaza was juxtaposed with 'ticketable' spaces that could generate revenue. Finding the right mix between commercial uses and users and the democratic rights of citizens to utilise this public urban space has always been a tricky balancing act. As discussed in Chapter Five, this is an issue that has vexed city planners internationally, most notably in the United States, where what became known as the 'crisis of the city' saw inner-city regions essentially abandoned in the 1970s and 1980s, with public spaces overtaken by the homeless, the mentally ill, criminals and the marginalised. Melbourne's old City Square suffered from some of these problems, although there it was often bored teenagers rather than the homeless who were perceived to be a public nuisance and a potential threat to other users of the space. In part because of this perception and in part because of bad design, the commercial tenancies and public gathering places there never really worked. The planners and managers of Federation Square were determined to avoid this fate for their new venture.

What became known as Federation Square's 'founding document', or what we might call its 'basic law', the Civic and Cultural Charter, was central to getting this process right. Devised in 1996 and 1997 and agreed to by all parties involved in creating Federation Square, this document sets out the various functions of the Square and provides guidelines for achieving them. It is prescriptive, but it also allows for flexibility in how the site is operated and managed. This chapter discusses the sometimes conflicting requirements of Federation Square, as set out in the Civic and Cultural Charter, and how the various roles and functions of the Square as both a public and a private space have been reconciled over the last 10 years. First we examine the charter in order to understand what it means and how it has been interpreted in practice. Then we look at the ownership and management structure of Federation Square to understand how this has involved a constant juggle for the management team as they have sought to maintain the financial stability of the commercial operations of the Square alongside an abiding commitment to its public and civic uses.

AFL Grand Final. Photo: David Simmonds

The Atrium at night. Photo: David Simmonds

The Upper Square. Photo: Marcel Aucar

Henna painting at The Light in Winter, 2010. Photo: Julie Renouf

THE CIVIC AND CULTURAL CHARTER

The Federation Square Civic and Cultural Charter was agreed between the Melbourne City Council and the Victorian Government as part of their negotiations on the planning and funding of the project. Its stated aims are to ensure that the Square contributes to Melbourne's 'pre-eminence as a centre for creativity and innovation', and that the city's diverse arts, cultural and immigrant communities 'find expression in Federation Square's management philosophy, marketing, programmed events and activities'. These roles are also required to be reflected in the Square's marketing and presentation and in the 'hiring and sub-leasing' of its commercial spaces. As in the design brief, the charter proclaims a number of 'key objectives' for Federation Square, mainly based on the idea that it was to become an important tourist hub and represent and showcase Melbourne's cultural and creative diversity to residents and local and international visitors. It was also to 'provide a focal point for arts and cultural festivals and activities and important civic commemorations'. 'Key outcomes', which would ensure that these objectives were achieved, include among others: 'a continuous and high calibre mix of cultural programming and civic activity that is recognised as contemporary and stimulating' as well as an 'identifiable synergy between the cultural program and other leisure, personal and commercial services'. The Square was also to be a safe place, 'an accessible, secure and public experience'.

Nine 'implementation requirements' define how the management company could achieve the social, cultural and financial objectives of the charter and specify the tasks that needed to be undertaken. Some of these requirements were relatively straightforward to meet, such as developing a 'year-round program of activities embracing visual, performing, multimedia, event, literary, festival, botanical, multicultural and other themes', while others

Australia Day, 2006. Photo: David Simmonds

Everfresh: Phibs, Rone, Maka, Meggs, Wonderlust and special guest Miso at NGV Studio, Photo: NGV Photographic Services

were to prove unachievable. Given the problems in constructing the Square, producing and promoting 'the celebration of the Centenary of Federation in 2001' in conjunction with the government and council was always going to be a tough ask, and so it turned out. Most of the other objectives were achieved, however, and continue to be adhered to today.

A number of clauses are built into the charter to ensure that Federation Square is not only accessible but also a safe and inviting place. The Civic Plaza is to be available for hire at 'market rates' to organisations for commercial purposes, and who those organisations are and how they present themselves and their products must be consistent with the ideals of the charter. Non-commercial groups, including arts and festival organisations and public sector agencies, are to be given access to the Civic Plaza at what is called 'nil hire cost', although they are required to pay for or provide assistance to cover costs such as insurance, power, security, set-up and dismantling, and similar tasks. In most cases, these groups and organisations are to be given priority in the use of the Square over commercial interests.

In order to ensure that the Square is a safe, secure place, the management company is expected to 'enforce rules and codes of public behaviour, and ensure an adequate level of the Square's uses by the public', but is given broad discretion in determining how to do this. Management are required to work with major cultural institutions to ensure an integrated program of events to attract visitors, and to link any special event at one venue with complementary ones at others. Commercial agreements, including the retail mix, must be determined by the management company as part of its remit to comply with the charter's insistence on an identifiable market niche. All terms and conditions of leases must be determined by the company in compliance with the charter. From the outset, attaining the highest rent was not necessarily the prime objective, although financial sustainability was a consideration. The charter stipulates that all retail outlets must 'embrace and enhance' the cultural and civic objectives of the Square, and all are expected to partake in and support special events and festivals. Federation Square is thus an integrated destination with a distinct social, cultural and commercial focus.

Earth Hour, 2008. Photo: David Simmonds

MANAGING THE SQUARE

The rules of the Civic and Cultural Charter mean that the guiding principles of the Square are different to those of a suburban or city centre shopping mall. Rather than simply seek to extract maximum sales and thus rental value from the tenancies, management are able to create a vision of what sort of 'experience' they want visitors to have, and to let space accordingly. Federation Square is publicly owned, but it is not a public place like a street or public garden. Instead it is privately operated and managed site, albeit one owned by a government-owned company. Fed Square Pty Ltd is a limited liability company wholly owned by State Trustees Limited as custodian trustee on behalf of the Government of Victoria. Its 'principal task' is to manage and maintain the Square, and to do so in accordance with the Civic and Cultural Charter, which is embedded in the company's constitution. The Victorian Government is the only shareholder and appoints a board of four directors – none of whom are government ministers or councillors of the City of Melbourne – to oversee the company's operations. The board has a range of responsibilities, mostly to do with ensuring that the company's

vision, mission, values and ethical standards are adhered to, and ensuring the Square's long-term viability and financial position. Day-to-day operations and management of the Square are conducted by the chief executive officer and a staff of about 40. The company operates on commercial principles and, other than the costs associated with building and finishing the Square between 1998 and 2003, it does not and has not received funding from the Victorian Government. The chief executive officer and staff have broad discretionary powers to decide what can happen on the Square's site, to decide what activities will be encouraged, and to ensure that the requirements of the Civic and Cultural Charter are adhered to.

The inclusion of The Ian Potter Centre: NGV Australia meant that the original design of the Square had to be inverted. This was both a challenge and a blessing: a challenge in that it meant that the architects had to revisit their design in order to accommodate a large and potential technically difficult building, but a blessing in that it created another major destination and hence crowd-attractor for the Square. The idea of incorporating the

Clockwise from left:

Commonwealth Games, 2006. Photo: David Simmonds

Melbourne Visitor Centre. Photo: David Simmonds

Labyrinth wall closeup.

gallery in the design proposal became a minor factor in the decision to award the winning bid to Lab Architecture Studio because, according to one of the judges, of all the shortlisted proposals, only this design with its 'campus' model of buildings arranged around the central civic space was easily adaptable to the new parameters. The adaptability of the Lab design, the number and variability of its buildings, and their ability to be rearranged if necessary was in the proposal's favour. Most of the other proposals, which featured only one or two buildings, were more monolithic in style and not so easily adaptable.

The final design switched ACMI and Cinemedia from the rear of the site to the Flinders Street frontage. This building was then replaced by The Ian Potter Centre: NGV Australia, which became the rear anchor and a 'magnet' that would draw people through the Square and past a number of other attractions. ACMI is housed in what is now known as the Alfred Deakin Building, named after an early Australian prime minister who hailed from Victoria. The Atrium links the gallery and Alfred Deakin Building and, in theory at least, acts as a visual drawcard into the site from the Hosier Lane restaurant and bar strip across Flinders Street. The fact that there is no safe place to cross Flinders Street along this axis, however, makes the crossing between the two destinations a very hazardous, not to mention illegal, endeavour. The 'ticketable' BMW Edge replaced the original Wintergarden proposal, and overlooks the Yarra River and the bay and southern suburbs beyond.

Other buildings include the Crossbar, which hosts restaurants at ground and second-floor levels, and corporate offices (including the Square's management company) in between. The Yarra Building encloses the site to the south and provides restaurant and other facilities, which look towards the Civic Plaza on one side and the river on the other. The Yarra Building also contains office space, while the Zinc building to the rear of BMW Edge is a multi-use hireable function space. One of the shards is now the Melbourne Visitor Centre, while the second acts as a western buffer to the Flinders Street Amphitheatre. Its distinctive slashed facade flashes messages and electronic information about the Square and other news and events. Transport Hotel faces Flinders Street Station across Swanston Street and also provides the backdrop to perhaps the Square's most famous and important feature, the Big Screen.

The other major components of Federation Square are the Labyrinth and the car park, both integral to the functioning of the site, but not prominent aspects of its public face. The Labyrinth is a 'maze of zig-zag surface corrugated concrete walls' between the deck and the surface of the Square. Almost 40 × 40 metres and 1.4 kilometres in length, the Labyrinth is an environmentally friendly air-conditioning system that provides cool air to the Atrium, BMW Edge and other parts of the Square in summer and warm air in winter. In summer, the system draws in cool air through the concrete cells at night, which helps to cool the concrete walls of the buildings during the day. The Labyrinth allows the air inside the Atrium and other internal areas to be up to 12 degrees Centigrade below that outside. In winter it creates a thermal air mass that can be used to supplement air-conditioning. The system uses about one-tenth of the energy used by conventional air-conditioning, which 'drastically reduces carbon emissions' and is cheaper to operate. The car park is also integral to the functioning of the Square in that it provides accessibility to visitors who do not have ready access to public transport, and because of the revenue it provides, which in most years is the Square's largest single source of income. In 2003, Federation Square was expanded to take in responsibility for the management of the bluestone storage vaults that have existed alongside the Yarra since the current Princes Bridge was built in 1888, as well as the river front itself, which has been renamed Federation Wharf.

Getting the right mix of tenants and ensuring that they work together to enhance the 'visitor experience' has been a key issue for Federation Square management since its opening in 2002. Former CEO Peter Seamer recalls that from the outset he was very conscious that if Melburnians were to take 'ownership' of the Square then it needed a broad range of offerings and attractions beyond those that mainly appeal to the cultural and artistic communities of the inner city. As we shall see in Chapter Four, one way of doing this in line with the charter was to open the Civic Plaza to community and multicultural groups. Another strategy was to ensure that the retail tenants were not too narrowly focussed. While bars and restaurants were always planned to be central to offerings, other possibilities discussed included a bookshop and a second-hand book market on Sundays, a museum dedicated to horse racing, and the cinemas associated with ACMI. Most of these except the bookshop came to fruition, and from the outset the Square has had a remarkably stable tenancy base. The major cultural institutions, The Ian Potter Centre: NGV Australia and ACMI, as well as SBS, have been there since the Square opened, as has the Melbourne Visitor Centre in the controversial western shard. From 2004 they were joined on the opposite side of the Civic Plaza by the Australian Racing Museum, although the evidence suggests that this attraction never really worked. It was relocated to the enlarged National Sports Museum at the MCG in 2009. Many of the commercial tenancies have been in place since the beginning, and it is perhaps their longevity that has contributed to the Square's continuing success as a popular destination for locals and visitors alike. Transport Hotel, which anchors the major building facing Swanston Street, acts as a major drawcard into the Square from the western side, while the Atrium,

Puppets at Fed Square, 2009. Photo: Marcel Aucar

SBS, Melbourne studios. Photo: John Gollings

Time Out Cafe.

The Light in Winter, 2010. Photo: Julie Renouf

The Light in Winter, 2010. Photo: Julie Renouf

The Light in Winter, 2011. Photo: Fred Kroh

Screen Worlds exibition at ACMI. Photo: Travis De Clifford

Melbourne International Arts Festival, 2004. Photo: David Simmonds

which has long had a beer and wine focus, does the same from the east. The Atrium is also important as a site of special events and festivals that showcase Victorian industries and products.

Current CEO Kate Brennan recognises that one of her key tasks is to maintain Federation Square's popularity and attractiveness to a broad range of people, while at the same time ensuring its financial sustainability. Her job and that of her team is to keep working on this mix and to ensure that each of these roles does not impinge too much on the other. Unlike other entertainment precincts, Federation Square must not and cannot become too dominated by liquor or by entertainment outlets where the emphasis is predominantly on alcohol consumption. And neither can it be a place where only the well-heeled can afford to eat and drink. Unlike some entertainment strips where an over-supply of bars and restaurants has led to a night-time-only economy aimed at an adult market, Federation Square must be both a day and a night destination. Most of its bars, restaurants and food outlets are required to be open day and night six or seven days per week. And, within

reason, they must also be friendly to a range of people and groups: families with children, teenagers and young adults, older people and locals and well as tourists.

Central to the experience of the Square is the Big Screen. As mentioned in Chapter Two, the Big Screen and ACMI were key components of the original plans for the Square, as was the desire to utilise the Civic Plaza for public gatherings and occasions. The screen does both of these things. Throughout its history, and at various times of the day and night, it has showcased major events within the Square itself and from places elsewhere in Melbourne, across Australia and around the world. It sometimes transmits curated cultural content, selected television programs, independent films and other media productions. The screen has also hosted live electronic gaming contests that have managed to attract a range of spectators watching from multiple vantage points around the Square. These various uses of the screen, and its visibility from so many spots around the Square, make it a major attraction. Like major cultural events, it acts as a magnet to visitors and those passing by.

The stage plays a similar role, hosting all sorts of formal and informal events, including bands and musicians, speakers and presentations. In line with the charter, the stage and the screen showcase Melbourne to the world. But both also act as a mirror for the city itself, especially its ethnic and social diversity. And in linking Melbourne to the world visually, the stage and the screen are at the same time highly local but also global spaces. As with any other hi-tech space, the screen and its technology must be kept up to date. Today's attractions might seem passé if not a complete embarrassment tomorrow, while content that simply replicates what can be seen on television will quickly lose its allure.

As with the Square's food, drink and retail mix, if the Big Screen and the stage are seen to be either too esoteric for the general public, or worse, simply advertising for commercial sponsors, then they will fail.

The task for Federation Square management remains as it has been since the days before it opened in 2002: how to reconcile the commercial imperatives of a large, diverse site with the social and cultural objectives of the Civic and Cultural Charter. It is also to ensure that Federation Square works as a destination in its own right, but that it is more than just another shopping mall or entertainment venue. Finding ways to make the Square attractive to its various users, while ensuring the Square's financial viability and fulfilling the requirements of the charter and the needs and desires of a range of visitor groups has been a difficult balancing act. Fortunately good management combined with public goodwill has so far meant that this has been achieved.

Australian Idol fans. Photo: David Simmonds

CHAPTER FOUR

MELBOURNE'S SQUARE

While the polarising design of Federation Square and the drawn-out saga of its completion meant that it had a mixed reputation upon opening, it soon became apparent that many Melburnians – whatever their doubts about its architecture – recognised it as an important and inviting civic space. With the demise of the City Square just up Swanston Street as a viable gathering and protest space after one half of the site was sold off for development and the other half manicured as mostly commercial recreational space dominated by cafes and restaurants, Federation Square soon became Melbourne's meeting place. The other increasingly popular spot, the lawns of the State Library of Victoria, even further up Swanston Street, became the bookend of a new informal 'civic spine'. Melbourne's long tradition as a city of protest meant that the latter became the meeting place for marches, with the Square the end point. Whereas once demonstrators marched from the Trades Hall or Melbourne University to Parliament, increasingly they meet at the State Library and march down Swanston Street to Federation Square.

But it is not only marchers and protestors who use the State Library lawns and Federation Square as meeting places. The increasing population of the CBD and surrounds, as well as the rapidly growing numbers of students in the inner city, mean that public places to meet, socialise and eat have become very important features of the 'new' city. The State Library lawns and Federation Square, linked by the traffic-free Swanston Street have become the front and backyards of the emerging vibrant, people-friendly Melbourne. From very early in its life Federation Square management utilised the imprimatur of the Civic and Cultural Charter to ensure that the Square did indeed become a community space and a showcase for the many communities and 'urban tribes' of Melbourne. The public in turn increasingly took it over as 'their' space, the natural gathering place in which to celebrate, watch and participate in sport and major political events, or to simply meet friends and relax. The Square's major cultural institutions also acted as people magnets, places to which locals and tourists were drawn when visiting the city centre. Blockbuster events, showcases and destination marketing strategies were in part responsible for this, but more recently it has become clear that for many locals Federation Square is becoming an integral part of the life of the city, somewhere that just is, rather than a special-occasions destination. For tourists and visitors it has become a 'must see' destination, part of the Melbourne and Australian experience. This chapter traces the evolution of Federation Square from something of a curiosity in its early years to its current status as central to Melbourne's view of itself, and that which it presents to the world.

Left: World Cup Soccer Qualifier, 2005. Photo: David Simmonds   Above: AFL Grand Final. Photo: David Simmonds

MAJOR EVENTS AND FEDERATION SQUARE

Federation Square's first major outing as a gathering space for events was New Year's Eve 2002, when it took over from Southbank, and before that the City Square, as the site of Melbourne's New Year street party and fireworks display. Having missed two planned opportunities to host the party in 2000 and 2001, the 2002 event saw thousands of people gather to witness the New Year's fireworks live in the Square and to watch others from around Australia and the globe do the same on the Big Screen. Federation Square's first public New Year's Eve party was a great success, but in reality this was actually its second Hogmanay outing, as a year previously a small but select group comprising members of the Federation Square team had gathered for a private party on the top floor of what was to become Transport Hotel to drink champagne and watch the Southbank fireworks. CEO Peter Seamer recalls that they all got soaked during a midnight downpour, but that everyone involved had a wonderful time, as they recognised just what was possible with this site. He also recalls thinking that next year the many thousands of people currently milling around St Kilda Road and locked out of the site by hoardings would be gathered in the Square itself. This was another of those occasions when he and his team knew that Federation Square would be a success.

The early months of 2003 were busy times for Federation Square, its tenants and the management team. As the restaurants, bars and galleries came on stream, and as more and more people began to recognise the possibilities of the Square, a series of planned and unplanned events saw its popularity dramatically increase. In January 2003, the Big Screen became an extension of Melbourne Park during the Australian Open tennis as crowds gathered to watch matches there, while on Australia Day national daytime celebrations were held for the first time in the Square during the tennis, fitting perhaps given that alongside Professor Fiona Stanley as Australian of the Year, tennis player Lleyton Hewitt was named Young Australian of the Year. Sport became increasingly important to Federation Square's public role over the next few years. September 2003 saw the AFL Grand Final played live on the screen for the first time, while a few weeks later large crowds gathered to watch Rugby World Cup matches live as they were played in cities across Australia and New Zealand. November also saw the Melbourne Cup Parade finish at the Square for the first time. Three years later, the Square was to be central to the success of the 2006 Melbourne Commonwealth Games. Again the Big Screen was important, as events were shown live, and the Square was popular as a central gathering place for local and visiting sports fans alike. The Square was the venue for a cultural festival staged alongside the Commonwealth Games, and more than 750,000 people visited over 10 days.

Homeless World Cup. Photos: David Simmonds

Apology Day, 2008. Photos: David Simmonds

In November 2005, thousands gathered to watch a screening of Australia playing Uruguay in Sydney in a successful bid to qualify for the FIFA World Cup finals in Germany in 2006. During that tournament the Square hosted huge night-time crowds as up to 10,000 people at a time gathered to watch matches televised on the Big Screen until the early hours of the morning. When Australia played Italy in the elimination round match, spillover spaces had to be opened in Birrarung Marr and elsewhere around the city. The crowds were so large that for safety reasons a decision was made to show all the 2010 matches in Birrarung Marr rather than in the Square. November 2008 saw both Federation Square and Birrarung Marr host matches of the Homeless World Cup, while in 2011 the Square combined celebrity and sport by being the venue for cyclist Cadel Evans' homecoming parade after he became the first Australian to win the Tour de France.

Perhaps the day that Federation Square came of age as a site of civic protest was on 14 February 2003. Less than six months after its opening, the Square saw its first major political rally as more than 100,000 people marched

to it from the State Library in protest against the looming prospect of war against Iraq. The *Age* reported it as possibly Melbourne's biggest ever peace rally, eclipsing the famous Vietnam War 'moratorium' march of May 1970. In Federation Square they were addressed by among others journalist John Pilger and former rock star Peter Garrett, who was then head of the Australian Conservation Foundation. On the Square's first anniversary later that year several people credited the Iraq protests with being the key moment when Melburnians naturally began to accept it as the city's new civic heart and thus the most appropriate place to voice their opinions. Demographer and urban commentator Bernard Salt suggested that the anti-war protests were a pivotal moment for the Square: 'Whether you are for the war or against it is irrelevant, the point is that it was the natural place of assembly for people wanting to exercise their democratic right. Where else could that have taken place? To me, that's a win,' argued Salt in the *Age* newspaper. Some Federation Square staff maintain to this day that 14 February 2003 was the day when the Square came into its own. Manager of Corporate Services Bill Blakeney

recalls a late-afternoon phone call informing management and staff that up to 200,000 people were heading their way. Along with other staff he had to make sure that they (and the Square) were safe. Others are not so sure about the impact of the Iraq protest on public perceptions of the Square. Former CEO Peter Seamer sees the open days during construction as much more important moments, suggesting that the Iraq protest has become mythologised in Federation Square history, mainly by those who were against the war and thus part of the mythology of the day. Who knows which is the truth, but certainly the images from that day are highly evocative.

Almost three years later, in November 2005, Federation Square was the starting point rather than the final destination of another massive demonstration, this time against the Howard government's proposed industrial relations laws, known as Work Choices. In driving rain, more than 150,000 people gathered in and around Federation Square to march to a rally in the Carlton Gardens. Again Federation Square's Big Screen was important as images from the rally were beamed live to other marches and demonstrations across the country. A follow-up rally a year later saw more than 50,000 people march from the MCG to Federation Square. But perhaps the Square's most notable political day came more than five years after its opening, when on 13 February 2008 it was one of the official national 'live sites' where people gathered to watch and listen to Prime Minister Kevin Rudd issue the formal Apology to the Stolen Generations of Aboriginal People. The *Age* reported that 'about 8000 people, including high school students and toddlers, filled Federation Square to witness the historic event' live on the Big Screen. The paper also reported that many witnesses shed tears as the prime minister spoke, and later turned their backs on opposition leader Brendan Nelson when he was seen to have politicised the occasion by lamenting the poor living and social conditions of contemporary Aboriginal people. Text messages in support of the apology and condemning Nelson's speech were televised on the Big Screen. Later that afternoon a free concert featuring Aboriginal performers including Archie Roach and Ruby Hunter was held on the main stage of the Square and broadcast live over the internet.

All of Us, 2008. Photo: David Simmonds

Cadel Evans, 2011. Photo: Janusz Molinski

Car Club Showcase. Photo: David Simmonds

Wine Showcase. Photo: Marcel Aucar

THE PEOPLE'S SQUARE

For politically minded people, Federation Square may well be remembered for hosting rallies and overtly political events, but for most people the Square is a site of culture, leisure and fun rather than protest. The management company's most recent media kit claims that more than 80 million people have visited since its opening 10 years ago, and that each year more than 2,000 events and activities – 40 per week – are held there. These range from festivals, markets, fashion shows and public lectures, to films, concerts and protests and rallies. Some of these are major government-sponsored and endorsed events such the Film Festival, the Writers Festival, the Arts Festival, the Comedy Festival, the Food and Wine Festival and the Fashion Festival, while others are more low-key community-based gatherings such as multicultural festivals and flag-raising ceremonies on national days. Literary and academic events such as conferences, speeches by local and international authors and speakers, as well as book and poetry readings are regular features of the Square's calendar, as is the weekly book market. Other regular events include a monthly car club showcase, weekly public tai chi exercises, a bi-monthly Victorian wine region showcase and a twice-yearly showcase of Victorian microbrewers. While some of these events have entry fees attached and are delivered on a commercial basis, in line with the Civic and Cultural Charter, a minimum of 70 per cent of public events at the Square are free, while 20 per cent are public but ticketed, and only 10 per cent are private and delivered on a commercial basis.

As mentioned above, Federation Square was the site for the cultural festival associated with the Commonwealth Games in March 2006. Wominjeka – the Koorie 'Welcome Place' and cultural centre – was based in the Square, while the Atrium hosted 'Tribal Expressions', an Indigenous business showcase. Other cultural events have included the 'Contemporary Commonwealth' showcase of art jointly sponsored by The Ian Potter Centre: NGV Australia and ACMI, and performances by artists, performers and musicians from around the Commonwealth. There were also nightly opportunities for the public to watch (and take part in) exhibitions of dancing from countries within the Commonwealth, including Fiji and India, and on St Patrick's Day a demonstration of Irish dancing.

High-profile and popular cultural events have also increased the visibility and use of the Square since its early years. The major cultural institutions such as The Ian Potter Centre: NGV Australia and ACMI are important in bringing people in, but so too were shorter-lived venues such as the Racing Hall of Fame and later the 'Abbaworld' exhibition. One-off events were also important. In August 2004, members of rock band Regurgitator spent three weeks living inside a specially constructed 'bubble' in Federation Square while recording their album *Mishmash*. The 'bubble' was open to view by the public and the band's activities – including sleeping and eating food prepared by band member Quan Yeoman's chef mother – were broadcast live on screens around the Square and onto a designated 24-hour TV channel on the Foxtel network. Three years later, in April 2007, Federation Square was the site of a semi-secret gig by three members of the Red Hot Chilli Peppers who performed for free in front of 3,000 fans as a warm-up before their official show at the Myer Music Bowl. Other major cultural events have included a televised 'masterclass' by filmmaker Tim Burton as part of an exhibition of his work at ACMI in 2010, which coincided with the 'Solar Equation', a giant lit-up balloon suspended over the Square as part of the annual 'The Light in Winter' celebration of the winter solstice. In 2008, the third international 'Urban Screens' conference was held at the Square as part of a joint research project between Fed Square and researchers in the School of Culture and Communications at the University of Melbourne. This project led in 2009 to an experiment that saw artists in Melbourne and

Songdo, South Korea, display their work live to the public in real time across continents via giant screens in the two cities.

It is not only major events and celebrations that bring people to Federation Square. The major cultural institutions are responsible for attracting large numbers of visitors, whether to see 'blockbuster' exhibitions or simply to see or experience art and culture. The cinemas and interactive spaces of ACMI bring in crowds, as do the restaurants and bars linked to these sites. People also come for the various cultural, creative and educational programs developed over the years as part of Fed Square management's commitment to make the Square a central component of Melbourne's civic and cultural life. A creative program seeks to cultivate 'unique artistic relationships, a diversity of new site-specific works throughout the year, and various forums for public engagement with artists'. The priority is to work with 'independent artists and producers who can initiate stimulating work that responds very specifically to the unique physical and social environment that is Federation Square'. Recent examples have included: 'Tape Melbourne', an interactive installation made entirely of packing tape in September 2011; 'In the Pines' by These Are The Projects We Do Together, which saw plastic Christmas trees re-used in a variety of installations and performances in December 2011; and Australian premieres of Strandbeest by renowned Dutch artist Theo Jansen and Stickwork by Patrick Dougherty. Federation Square also acts as an 'incubator, enabler and host for a range of arts festivals and initiatives' throughout the year.

The educational program evolved out of the original idea of Federation Square as a civic place that celebrates the centenary of Australian Federation. While the proposed Federation exhibition that was originally planned to be housed in the east shard never went ahead, Federation and the broader history of Australia is told in the 'Federation Story' exhibition located on the balcony of the Atrium. A larger, evolving program, 'Fed Ed', is aimed at school students and involves a number of activities and projects that draw on the facilities and resources of the Square and its major institutions to allow students to explore the ethics, intercultural understandings, civics, histories and cultures of various groups, including Indigenous Australians, and Australia's engagement with Asia. Maths and science subjects are also taught, again by drawing on the resources of the major institutions, especially ACMI. The educational programs are linked to the various festivals, including 'The Light in Winter', the Melbourne Writers Festival and others, and are designed to show that education and community and civic engagement are interlinked rather than separate endeavours. Again, this is an example of Federation Square's various civic, community and cultural roles coming together in all sorts of interesting ways.

The Square has also become Melbourne's 'front garden', the place where it puts on its best face to the world. The annual AFL Grand Final Parade now ends at the Square, as does the Melbourne Cup Parade. New Year's Eve is celebrated there as is Australia Day and, reflecting the Square's commitment to promoting multiculturalism, festivals and celebrations of a huge variety of ethnic and national days. Federation Square has become the natural place to host visiting dignitaries and celebrities such as Queen Elizabeth II, who visited in 2011 and the queen of daytime television Oprah Winfrey who was feted at a major public event as part of her 'Down Under' tour in 2010. Long before Federation Square welcomed home Cadel Evans in 2011, it had played the same role for athletes returning from Commonwealth and Olympic Games in 2004, 2008 and 2010. Cricketers playing in the annual Boxing Day Test at the MCG regularly greet fans at the Square, as do other sporting people. The Square and the Big Screen are also used as a means of including people in memorials and services that are not readily accessible to large crowds. In 2009, the memorial service for victims of the Victorian bushfires was screened there, and in 2012 the Square provided space and a viewing spot for grieving fans who were unable to fit inside St Paul's Cathedral opposite the Square for the state funeral service of football hero and community worker, the late Jim Stynes.

Tape Melbourne, 2011. Photo: Fred Kroh

Above: A message left on the paving stones during the rally against the Iraq War, 2003. Photo: Julie Renouf

Left: Thousands gather at Federation Square for the Valentine's Day Peace Rally. Photo: Stuart Milligan, Fairfax Syndication

Queen Elizabeth II, 2011. Photo: John Gollings

The Australia Olympic team, home from Beijing, 2008. Photo: Julie Renouf

People come for a variety of other reasons, and Federation Square has become a kind of 'village green' for the city. Visitor and customer satisfaction surveys taken within the Square and by phone and other polling allow us to track the number of times Victorians have visited Federation Square since 2005, why they did so and how they rated their visit. By 2005, three years after its opening, more than 70 per cent of Victorians had visited the Square, a figure that by 2007 had climbed to more than 90 per cent. The number who think the Square is Melbourne's 'major community focal point' has been growing steadily. Whereas in 2004 only 47 per cent of respondents agreed with this statement, by 2012 that figure had climbed to 84 per cent. Similar numbers saw the Square as helping to 'attract interstate and overseas visitors to Melbourne and Victoria'.

In both 2005 and 2011, the average annual number of visits by Victorians was about 3.6, although this number hides spikes in 2005 and 2007 when it was above 5.3 and 5.5 respectively, and differences based on place of residence, age and gender. As would be expected, Melburnians were much more likely to visit more often than people from regional areas, although in the earlier years this was not as pronounced as it has become more recently, perhaps reflecting the Square's initial novelty value or possibly its role in the Commonwealth Games. For most people, whether male or female, however, the major reason to visit was listed as 'just looking/walking around/general sightseeing'. The other major attractions were the galleries, food and drink, and events and activities. Perhaps surprisingly, the numbers of male and female visitors were roughly the same. Whether they visit for the same reasons, is of course debatable. It is possible that women come to visit the galleries and museums, while the men may be greeting sports stars and sampling the beer and wine, or perhaps ogling the vintage cars.

People under 30 (whether male or female) are far more regular visitors than older people, perhaps reflecting the increasing popularity of the bars and restaurants, but perhaps because of the major sporting and cultural events as well. It may also reflect the Square's growing reputation as the place for young people to meet up before going out to bars and clubs elsewhere in

Visitors taking advantantage of the Square's free wi-fi. Photo: David Simmonds

Transport Hotel. Photo: Rhiannon Slatter

the city centre. There is some evidence that Federation Square has overtaken the stairs 'under the clocks' at Flinders Street Station as Melbourne's meeting place. Whatever the reason, under 30s are by far the largest users of the Square and their use of it is growing. Whereas up until 2008 their average number of visits was only slightly more than that of their elders, by 2011 that figure had shot up dramatically to more than 65 per year for the under 20s and to 35 for those aged 20–29, almost double that of those in their 30s and significantly higher than those in the older age groups. All of this suggests that, as might be expected, the various venues of Federation Square have become an integral component of younger Melburnians' nightlife scene.

In the 10 years of its existence so far, Federation Square has thus grown from being a bit of a novelty to very quickly becoming central to Melbourne and its sense of itself. In part this process has been helped along by a determined management group, who have sought to locate the Square centrally in the minds of Melburnians as 'their' space, the central civic place that the city has always wanted, but could never quite get right. The Civic and Cultural Charter helped this process as it relegated commercial considerations to second- or third-tier concerns for the management group, although they were still required to ensure the Square did not run at a loss. And so far it has worked. As mentioned in Chapter Three, the right mix of tenants has helped, but so too has a rather benign attitude towards uses that might have conflicted with a more commercial approach. As the Square has become more accepted and natural, the mix of events-oriented and more passive uses has had to change. Too many events with too big an audience may 'crowd out' the regular users, but the wrong mix of regulars might also inhibit casual visitation. So too might an overly strong emphasis on civic uses detract from the commercial imperatives of the various businesses and the Square's management company. Finding and maintaining the line between private and commercial needs and the right of the people to public space is an ongoing balancing act that in Federation Square, as in a number of other places internationally, is constantly renegotiated.

Australia Day, 2008. Photo: David Simmonds

CHAPTER FIVE

MANAGING THE PUBLIC SQUARE

As we saw in Chapter Three, Federation Square is a space that is owned by the public through the Victorian Government but it is managed and operated by a private company Fed Square Pty Ltd. The Square is governed by a charter that says it must operate in the public interest but it is also expected to be self-financing and not become a drain on the public purse. It is not required to generate profits, but it is expected to be financially sustainable now and into the future. The charter also says that the Square must be open and accessible to the public as a civic meeting and gathering space, but also a safe place where the myriad social, cultural, ethnic and demographic groups that make up Melbourne's population must feel welcome and safe. How to achieve these goals has been a challenge to Federation Square's managers over the years. In dealing with these issues of accessibility and financial sustainability, however, they are not alone. The 'right to the city' and access to public space are issues that have vexed city planners and governments for centuries, most especially since the rise of the mass city in the nineteenth century. More recently, the desire and the need to reinvent and revitalise city centres in the wake of the collapse of the old manufacturing-based economy has seen planners and urban governments grapple with the tensions between the economic needs of the leisure and tourist-oriented 'spectacle' city and the rights of all citizens to the spaces and facilities of the city, which after all they pay for through taxes.

This chapter explores the tensions between the social and political functions of Federation Square as a public space and how it fits into the role now played by the city centre as a driver of social, cultural and economic development for the wider metropolitan area, the state and indeed the nation. The chapter also examines the everyday operating practices of the Square's management team and the strategies they employ to balance these diverse audiences and needs. These are important questions that are not unique to Federation Square. Other public places around the world are examined to see how these issues are handled (or sometimes mishandled) elsewhere. This is related to some of the themes explored in Chapter One, which discusses the emergence of the 'new' post-industrial inner Melbourne that has emerged since the 1980s.

This chapter looks at international debates about the 'crisis of the city' in the 1960s and 1970s and then at more recent debates about both 'the right to the city' and about just who 'owns' the city in the contemporary post-industrial period. Federation Square and the questions around it can be seen as part of an international phenomenon that has its roots in the United States in the 1960s, but which is now being discussed in a range of cities and countries across the world.

Rally against Work Choices, 2005. Photo: David Simmonds

Photo: Marcel Aucar

THE CRISIS OF THE CITY

The rise of the car and the car-based suburb created all sorts of difficulties for cities, especially inner cities in the postwar years. The 'automobilisation' of society in this period meant that across the Western world people could live virtually wherever they wanted within a rapidly expanding metropolitan area, and yet still have access to the jobs, education and leisure facilities of the central city. In the Australian case, suburban living had been a feature of Australian cities from the outset of colonisation in the eighteenth and nineteenth centuries, but as Graeme Davison has shown in his recent book *Car Wars* these tendencies were compounded by the growing use of cars in the second half of the twentieth century. No longer reliant on the fixed routes of public transport facilities to get to work, Australians, like their North American cousins, followed their suburban dreams until by the 1970s most families owned at least one car and more than 70 per cent of Australians either owned or were buying homes. In Melbourne and most other Australian cities more than 75 per cent of these were detached houses on their own blocks. Australian cities were thus some of the most sprawling in the world, with very low residential and population densities. And as employees and customers moved away from the centre of town many businesses decided it was in their best interests to follow them. Hence the rise of the suburban shopping centre,

university and business park in the 1960s and 1970s. As discussed in Chapter One, in Melbourne this process saw the decline of the inner city as a place of residence and work. It also saw the collapse of the inner city as Melbourne's premier leisure and shopping destination as department stores, cinemas, pubs and theatres closed down in rapid succession in this period. By the 1980s there was talk of the 'doughnut city', heavily populated and thriving at the periphery but empty in the centre.

While there was some truth to these claims in Melbourne (and indeed to a lesser extent cities in Europe, especially England), in reality the doughnut city was a concept that was imported without much thought from the United States where a genuine crisis of the city – reflecting a major breakdown in the economic social and racial profile of major urban areas – became starkly evident in the 1960s and 1970s. There the coming of the car combined with various government initiatives to support home ownership among returned service personnel, racist restrictions on residency of non-whites and a massive program of freeway building that tore through older neighbourhoods and regions to see inner cities dramatically transformed in the postwar years. As white middle-class people left the inner cities for the suburbs, they were either replaced by poor African-Americans or in many cases not replaced at all. As

in Australia, population dropped rapidly in America's inner cities in the 1950s and 1960s, and later as jobs either migrated to the suburbs or in the 1970s overseas, the employment base of the inner city collapsed. As a consequence, America's inner city residents increasingly became more Black and Hispanic, poor, female and unemployed or underemployed. And in a political system in which education and other services are funded at the local level through city-based income and property taxes, the collapse of population and in turn the economic base meant that the capacity of cities to service the needs of these people decreased. The result was a spiral downwards, in which those who could leave did, leaving behind those with the most (and therefore most expensive) social and other problems. Riots in the late 1960s followed by de-industrialisation in the 1970s and government spending cuts in the 1980s exacerbated these problems until by the mid-1980s many American inner cities were essentially abandoned no-go areas.

A further public policy change in the United States, Australia and elsewhere in the 1970s and 1980s exacerbated the problems of the inner city. The closure of large and decrepit mental health institutions in this period was conceived as a humanitarian gesture that would see people who had previously been locked away returned to their communities for care and support. Instead, budget cuts and gentrification saw many of these people become homeless or living precarious existences in boarding and rooming houses. Many found themselves living on the streets without social or medical support. Inevitably they drifted to public parks and gathering places, further alienating the broader society from the city centre, which was increasingly seen as dangerous and threatening. In New York City, Times Square, Union Square and Grand Central Station became havens for the homeless, as did Central Park. These places also became centres for drug dealing, sex work, street crime and begging. Similar trends occurred in other cities internationally, and again this led to a spiral downwards. As public places became associated with homelessness, vice and crime the general public began to stay away, thus compounding the problem. Increasingly the people who ventured into these places were those who had either nowhere to else go or were up to no good. The broader population retreated to the suburbs, especially to suburban shopping malls and multiplex cinemas. Those who did venture into the city centre sought safety, comfort and protection from the elements in enclosed, blanked-wall and privately managed city centre shopping malls that became a feature of many cities in the 1980s. Melbourne's own example of this is Melbourne Central, which was deliberately oriented to turn its back on the street outside. As in the United States, this essentially amounted to a privatisation of what was once public space. These places were privately owned, privately managed and thus able to restrict who could enter and what they did while inside. As private sector organisations their owners' major imperative was to get people to spend money rather than protest or gather for political or other purposes.

Photo: Marcel Aucar

GENTRIFICATION AND THE NEW INNER CITY

While many who could were retreating from the increasingly threatening inner city in this period, a small but influential group were doing the opposite. The reduction in demand for inner-city property in this era opened up spaces for people with low incomes but high cultural capital to colonise city centres by buying up and renovating cheap old houses, especially where these were near important cultural institutions such as universities and colleges. In 1963, British urban sociologist Ruth Glass coined the term 'gentrification' to describe this process of urban inversion and recolonisation of the inner city by the wealthy, but in reality this is a process that had been underway in a number of cities in the English-speaking world since at least the 1920s. The wealthy have always lived in the centres of European and Latin American cities rather than in the suburbs. The best example of this process is Greenwich Village in New York which became an artistic and cultural quarter in the interwar years, but so too did Chelsea in London as to a lesser extent did St Kilda in Melbourne and Kings Cross in Sydney.

Two years before Glass, American sociologist Jane Jacobs had sung the praises of the small-scale shopping and friendliness of her Greenwich Village neighbourhood in New York and compared and contrasted it with what she saw as both the dullness of suburbia and the monumentalism of the new public housing blocks and freeway overpasses of the contemporary Modernist

city. Later, another sociologist Sharon Zukin documented the movement of artists into former manufacturing and industrial spaces in New York's SoHo and conversion of these spaces for residential and artistic use. Her book *Loft Living* told the story of artists and what we now call the 'creative class' who colonised the abandoned lofts of Manhattan's SoHo district in the 1970s and the tensions that developed between the needs of these people for cheap living and working spaces and those of owners and developers hungry to capitalise on the development potential of these well-located buildings. The result was what she called a 'cultural compromise', which saw culture and the arts become central to the new post-industrial economy of New York in the 1980s and beyond. Before long, the lofts became highly prized residential units, which today command prices in the millions. Needless to say, emerging artists can no longer afford to live there.

In a later book, Zukin wrote of the increasing importance that culture – high and popular – began to play in the economies of cities in the 1980s and 1990s. *The Culture of Cities* surveyed the emergence of culture as a driver of economic development in cities and the role that formal and informal 'cultural zones' play in the tourism-oriented post-industrial city of the late twentieth century. As she noted, 'with the disappearance of local manufacturing industries and periodic crises in government and finance, culture is more and more the business of cities [and] the basis of their tourist attractions and their unique, competitive edge'. As with gentrification, de-industrialisation and the increasing importance of culture to the economics of the city became a worldwide trend in the 1980s and 1990s. From François Mitterrand's *Grand Projets* in Paris to the Guggenheim Museum in Bilbao, governments sought to revitalise their cities' appeal to international investors and tourists by either building new or rejuvenating existing cultural facilities. Sport too became central to urban economics in this period, hence the increasing competition to host major events such as the World Cup soccer finals, the Olympics Games, and in the former British Empire, the Commonwealth Games. Sport and culture bring investment dollars, construction jobs and most importantly tourists and their money. As mentioned in Chapter One, these ideas quickly came to Australia and were central to Victorian Government economic strategies in this period.

WHOSE CITY?

As both Sharon Zukin and geographer David Harvey have suggested, the needs of the various groups that make up the new inner city can sometimes stand in sharp contrast and indeed conflict. Low income earners and the homeless need access to cheap or affordable and safe housing, while gentrifiers seeking an 'authentic' urban experience can pay current owners higher purchase prices and landlords higher rents. Wealthier owner–occupiers have different social and cultural tastes to renters, while artists and others find themselves constantly on the move as they are outpriced by both cashed-up home buyers and property developers seeking to make a quick buck converting factories to warehouse apartments. Younger residents seek out exciting (and noisy) nightlife, while older residents want quiet in order to get some sleep. Local business owners are priced out of their premises by chain stores, and

businesses selling cheap second-hand goods to niche bohemian markets such as students and artists find themselves competing with high-cost fashion boutiques aimed at the newer and richer gentrifiers. And all find themselves doing battle with tourists and the tourism industry that can outmuscle and outprice them all. David Harvey has recently suggested that in New York the process of gentrification and the remaking of the city has come to its logical conclusion, with Manhattan having become in recent years 'one vast gated community' increasingly only accessible to the rich and tourists. Zukin is not quite so forthright, but in both the *Culture of Cities* and more recently in the *Naked City* she does question the increasing bourgeoisification of New York and by extension other gentrifying cities. Along with Harvey, she also questions just who the new city is for, and thus who has the economic ability to access its new and renewed cultural facilities? Does the gentrification of the inner city and the increasing emphasis on locating cultural facilities there rather than in the less well-off outer zones, reinforce privilege and further entrench economic and social division?

Many of these questions about the new inner city are applicable to Melbourne, although here the divide between rich and poor and between different neighbourhoods is nowhere near as extreme as it is in the United States. But one of the key arguments in *Naked City* is possibly relevant to Melbourne and especially to the role of Federation Square. In a chapter entitled 'Union Square and the paradox of public space' Zukin draws attention to the increasing tendency in New York and elsewhere in the United States for the management and control of what were previously public spaces and streets to be handed over to what are known as partnerships, business improvement districts, local development corporations or 'park conservancies'. Mostly dominated by local business groups, these organisations invest time and money into improving the look and ambience of parks, neighbourhoods or

Photo: Carbie Warbie

Photo: Andrew Hobbs

shopping streets in order to make them more attractive to locals, visitors and tourists. By making these places feel safer and controlling what occurs and who can be within their parameters, they can increase the value of property nearby and increase the profitability of local businesses. But by being able to dictate who uses these formerly public spaces and what they do there, these private organisations have been allowed to take on many of the roles, such as controlling behaviour and enforcing law and order, that were formerly the responsibility of democratically elected governments. Some spaces such as Union Square (near Greenwich Village) have been reasonably tolerant of protesters, musicians and other public uses, while others such as the 125th Street (Harlem) Business Improvement District are less accommodating of non-commercial activities and enforce a much stricter behavioural regime, more akin to that of a private shopping mall than a public street.

Perhaps closer to the Federation Square experience is Millennium Park, located between the city and the waterfront in Chicago. Like Federation Square, it was a planned as a grand urban renewal project that would be opened in time to celebrate a major anniversary, but it too was delayed and was not finished until 2004. It also shares with Federation Square a Big Screen and an emphasis on striking and provocative architectural features. It is anchored by major cultural institutions and is subject to various rules and by-laws that are enforced by a private security company. Like Federation Square, it has been a great success, playing host to more than 500 annual events and 3.5 million visitors per year since its opening. But there are major differences between the two, the most important being that, unlike Federation Square, which was fully funded by the public sector, many of Millennium Park's major buildings and institutions were paid for by private philanthropists and companies. These institutions and structures bear the names of their benefactors, for example the BP Bridge, the Boeing Galleries and the Chase Promenade. Also unlike Federation Square, which emphasises public use and users over commercial imperatives, Millennium Park actively promotes itself as venue for hire for private, especially corporate, functions. Another important difference is that Millennium Park is not a place of protest; while technically legal it is discouraged by management, in part by insisting that any gathering of more than 50 people requires a permit.

Similar semi-public, semi-private developments have occurred elsewhere around the world, especially in English-speaking countries where governments have adopted neo-liberal or free-market oriented policies in recent decades. Privatisation has not only seen formerly government-owned trading assets sold off to the private sector, but public land and space as well. In London, Trafalgar Square remains a public place, but protest and use is strictly controlled by the Greater London Authority, which lets it out for commercial and other purposes on a case-by-case basis. It also polices protests and behaviour in and around the square. Pasternoster Square beside St Paul's Cathedral and the home of the London Stock Exchange, and the site of the Occupy London protest in 2011, is a privately owned open space and hence the protest and occupation there – unlike its equivalent in New York – technically involved trespass onto private property and was thus illegal. Further north, Liverpool One is an open-air residential, shopping and entertainment precinct that looks and feels like a series of ordinary city streets but is in fact owned and operated by a private company. The streets of Liverpool One are open to the public as 'rights of way' and are subject to municipal by-laws, but ultimately all activity, including visitor behaviour, is managed and controlled by a private company, Grosvenor Estates.

Individual views on whether the privatisation of these formerly public spaces is a good thing or not probably reflect personal politics and ideological values. But, as with many urban issues, including environmental ones, these are not necessarily questions that are easily divided along standard political lines and they can make for some rather odd political alliances. Access to public space and the voicing of dissent within that space is without question a democratic right. But so too is safety and the ability to use public spaces without fear of being assaulted or subjected to unwanted harassment. In the period of the crisis of the city, all sorts of people had access to the streets and parks, but their behaviour (whether consciously or not) made those spaces unattractive and potentially off limits to many others, especially women and families with children. An insistence by some people and groups to the untrammelled right to behave in any way they liked limited the right of others to equally use that space. While much of the fear associated with the city in those days was probably unfounded, there is no doubt that certain areas were dangerous, were uninviting and were thus unusable by a number of people. The new city is without question safer and more attractive to wealthier residents and tourists alike, but in being so it is also safer and more attractive to many others as well. Where is the line drawn between what is public space and private space, between the wants and needs of the local neighbourhood and rights of access of the broader community, between public access and commercial viability? And when does protest and dissent become public nuisance?

These are questions that have been central to the operations of Federation Square since before it opened 10 years ago. The Civic and Cultural Charter says that the Square must be accessible to as broad a constituency as possible but also that it must be financially sustainable. Federation Square is a civic space where protest is not only deemed acceptable but encouraged, but it is also a place of culture, business and commercial activity. It is a place where all of Melbourne's urban tribes and local and international tourists are welcomed, but also where bad or antisocial behaviour, especially that which interferes with others' use of the Square, is not acceptable or tolerated. Ultimately it is a public space that is owned and managed by what is essentially a private company. How then are these possibly conflicting roles reconciled? Both former CEO Peter Seamer and his successor Kate Brennan are acutely conscious of the responsibilities involved in managing these different roles. Seamer sees the private structure and control as central to the success of the Square, as it has allowed an integrated approach to its various functions. No one role is allowed to dominate. Brennan agrees, but recognises that this is an evolving process and that the management team must remain vigilant to ensure that the Square's offerings are constantly updated to cater to the needs and desires of its various target markets.

In order to avoid the fate of the privatisation and commercialisation of public spaces such as has occurred in New York, London and Liverpool, and to a lesser extent Chicago, Federation Square must remain a place that is inviting, safe and open, but that is above all about the community and the people rather than commerce. It needs to be a place for formal and informal gatherings – whether cultural, sporting, political or social – but it must also be a passive recreation space, a place where people can gather to simply sit and relax or meet up with friends. But gathering with friends can mean different things to different people. What may seem like innocent horseplay to teenagers can seem threatening and antisocial to older people. Sports fans celebrating their team's success can easily be mistaken for drunken hooligans by those not interested in sport, and legitimate protest about local or international issues can often be construed as unacceptable vandalism and violence when seen from some angles, especially on the Big Screen. And when any of these things involve people of a different social or ethnic group, all sorts of misunderstandings can happen. This is especially the case in a city as ethnically and socially diverse as Melbourne. Federation Square must be a place where everyone feels welcome, including the marginalised and the homeless. But again, in order for it to be a welcoming place to all, it cannot be a place of refuge or somewhere to sleep rough. Federation Square staff monitor the behaviour of visitors, and also work closely with welfare and other agencies such as the Salvation Army to ensure that services are available for those who need them. When prompted to speak on the multiple functions of the Square, Kate Brennan commented that it must be an 'empathetically managed space', and that one of the major roles of management is to balance the rights and needs of all the competing interests associated with Federation Square and to make sure that everyone has a sense of ownership and thus feels welcome there.

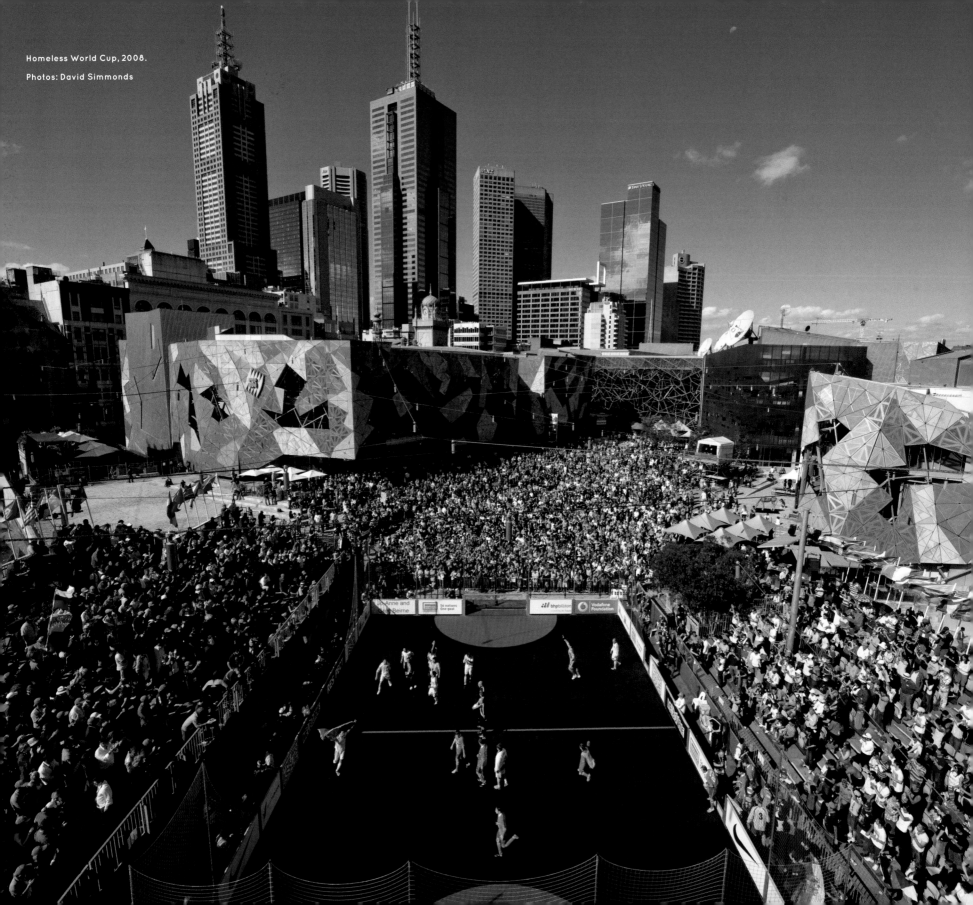

Homeless World Cup, 2008.

Photos: David Simmonds

Melbourne International Arts Festival, Merce Cunningham, 2007. Photo: David Simmo

CONCLUSION
THE NEXT 10 YEARS

As it moves into its second decade and beyond, Federation Square faces the opportunities and dilemmas that all innovative ideas and spaces face as they age. Once their novelty value wears off, how do they retain their popularity and distinctiveness, especially in a city as rapidly changing as Melbourne? Growing old gracefully while not sinking into irrelevance is something that all of us face, but few of us get right. This is especially true for places that are as exotic and controversial as Federation Square. How to avoid the future predicted by Barry Humphries and Miles Lewis in which Federation Square suffers the indignity of being seen as an embarrassing folly, or worse, a time capsule of monumental architectural ideas like its predecessor on the site, Princes Plaza, is a real challenge that is recognised by all involved in creating and managing the Square. Getting the future right is as important as was getting the thing up in the first place.

Fed Square CEO Kate Brennan and her team constantly tweak the face and mix of Federation Square's offerings and facilities so it appeals to new groups while retaining its popularity with the old. As the Square becomes more accepted as a part of Melbourne life and leisure, major events and structured community occasions may need to give way to more passive recreational uses in order to ensure high levels of return visitation, especially by locals. The emphasis on festivals and formal 'destination' events, while really useful in creating a sense of ownership for Melburnians, has the potential to inhibit more casual visitation. There is a possibility that Federation Square may be seen as the place to go to for big events rather than somewhere that is simply part of the city visit 'menu'.

Some subtle changes, such as the introduction of deckchairs and shade umbrellas, have already had an impact by making the Square less harsh in summer and more inviting as a place to sit out in during the day. Some further protection from the rain and cold while maintaining the architectural integrity of the original design may also be necessary, as will constant updates of offerings and exhibitions at the major cultural institutions. Perhaps the biggest challenge is that which has always faced Federation Square and its supporters, and that is the design of the Square itself. While many of us now recognise its architectural merits, some prominent critics still see it as a folly. In 2009, it came fifth in a survey of the 'world's top ugly buildings', while more recently a British survey rated it as number eight. Interestingly, however, feedback from Melburnians on these surveys has changed dramatically over the years. While 10 years ago many might have agreed with these findings the most recent survey saw a backlash from locals who defended it in the letters

Federation Square riverside. Photo: David Simmonds

and comments pages of both the *Age* and the *Herald Sun*. So while some critics still hate it, more observers have come to recognise and respect the subtleties and intricacies of its design and layout. Whether the materials used in cladding the various structures will date is, however, still open to debate. Either way, moves are already underway to have Federation Square nominated for heritage protection and listing, first at state level and then nationally.

Beyond that, who knows? Whether such listing will require the reinstatement of the original design of the shards is possibly a discussion for the future.

The other major issue for any innovative and hi-tech place or space is that what is futuristic today can seem very old-fashioned tomorrow. This is a problem in architecture but much more so in the world of media and information and communications technology. Big screens are the international rage right now, but in a world of ubiquitous information available at our fingertips will they be so in the future? Possibly not, but there is ample evidence that the 'atomising' processes of the internet and personal media devices actually increase our need to be with other people. That is why so many people come together in Federation Square to protest or assert our democratic rights and why so many of us gather there in the middle of the night in order to watch sport together rather than stay in the comfort and warmth of our homes. As public spaces that are open to all and provide the ground to meet and interact with our fellow citizens, Federation Square and places like it can be the glue that keeps society together especially during hard economic times.

Ethan Kent from the New York-based Project for Public Spaces organisation has described Federation Square as 'one of the boldest and most successful new public spaces in the world', arguing that in building and nurturing Federation Square Melbourne 'has gone further than any city in recent history in realising the potential for a central square to serve as a major civic and cultural destination'. In providing a central and accessible 'anchor' place for Melbourne, the Square not only helps to 'grow the community and cultural identity of the city', it is also serves to 'effectively showcase that identity to the world'. As with the broader revitalisation of the central city in recent years, the success of Federation Square has been a managed process that has been designed to enhance the economic and tourism potential of Melbourne. This has worked because it has been allowed to evolve to reflect the changing culture of the city around it rather than imposing on and resisting input from the various communities that use it. Its success has been a result of working with and trusting these communities to recognise and respect the importance to society of civic and public spaces rather than excluding them and actively policing their behaviour. The various festivals, gatherings, educational programs and public events that are such a feature of

Federation Square demonstrate that this is a place that is for everybody, not just the select few.

The cities that are most likely to be successful in the twenty-first century are those that encourage and enable the development or enhancement of spaces and events that make people feel good about themselves and allow them to celebrate the fact that they are part of a larger community, whether local, national or global. In part that success will be because in the post-industrial era fun and spectacle are drivers of economic growth. But sustainable economic success also requires people to have a sense of belonging. The places that have had the most difficulty in making the transition to the new economy are those that have gone too far down the path of valuing privacy and individualised consumption over the rights and responsibilities of the public realm. The other unsuccessful places are those that treat the public domain as just like any other business – over-designed in order to part visitors from their money. No-one wants to visit a dangerous public space, but nor do we get much lasting satisfaction from visiting yet another cookie-cutter shopping mall. Neither of these models are healthy for the democratic city.

The most important challenge for Federation Square and other spaces like it, then, is to ensure that it remains a democratic space, socially as well as politically. The right to protest there needs be upheld, but so too must the right to the city and its spaces and facilities be nurtured and protected. Federation Square and inner Melbourne more generally must not be allowed to become another of David Harvey's 'vast gated communities' accessible only to the wealthy and to tourists. Given the importance of the Civic and Cultural Charter to Federation Square and the way it has been observed and continues to be observed, that is never likely to happen. Perhaps then it is the charter rather than the Square itself that should be granted heritage status? After all, Federation Square is just a series of buildings, but the charter is about the people who use it.

Commonwealth Games, 2006. Photo: David Simmonds

NOTES ON SOURCES

INTRODUCTION

For an earlier study on Federation Square's site and architecture see Norman Day and Andrew May, *Federation Square*, Hardie Grant, Melbourne, 2003. Sharon Zukin's books on cities and culture include *Loft Living: Culture and Capital in Urban Change*, Johns Hopkins University Press, Baltimore 1982, *The Culture of Cities*, Blackwell, Cambridge (Mass), 1995 and *The Naked City: The Death and Life of Authentic Urban Places*, OUP, New York, 2010. On Harvey and Fordism, post-Fordism and the new city, see among others David Harvey *The Condition of Postmodernity: An Enquiry into the Origins of Cultural Change*, Wiley-Blackwell, Oxford, 1989 and the more recent *Rebel Cities: From the Right to the City to the Urban Revolution*, Verso, New York, 2012.

CHAPTER ONE

For a more detailed discussion of these processes of change in Melbourne and elsewhere see Seamus O'Hanlon, *Melbourne Remade: The Inner City Since the Seventies*, Arcade, Melbourne, 2010 and 'The events city: Sport, culture and the transformation of inner Melbourne, 1977–2006', *Urban History Review*, Vol. XXXVII, No. 2, 2009. The two reports on inner Melbourne's problems published in 1977 were *Melbourne's Inner Area: A Position Statement* produced by the MMBW, and *Socio-economic Implications of Urban Development*, which was written for the board by Urban Economic Consultants. On

Detroit's decline see Julien Temple (director), *Requiem for Detroit*, 2009. The Cain government's economic strategy was set out in *Victoria: The Next Step, Economic Initiatives and Opportunities for the 1980s* (1984). Rob Jolly reflected on these ideas in an interview in April 2008. 'Agenda 21' projects were set out in a series of brochures and pamphlets published throughout the mid-to-late 1990s, including the *Agenda 21 Quarterly* put out by the Public Office Branch of the Office of Major Projects. The Birrell quote is from Issue 8, December 1995. The figures for changes in central Melbourne's population, employment and visitation come from earlier studies by the author noted above and a City of Melbourne profile at: <www.melbourne.vic.gov.au/AboutMelbourne/MelbourneProfile/Pages/CityofMelbourneprofile.aspx>.

CHAPTER TWO

The information on the proposed Centenary Centre comes from interviews with Andrew Friend on 11 April 2012 and Rob Adams on 12 April 2012. See also City of Melbourne, 'The Centenary Centre: Gateway to the Melbourne experience', *c.* 1994. The quotes from Neville Quarry, Nigel Flanagan and Jeff Kennett about the winning design come from the *Herald Sun*, 28 and 29 July 1997. The Miles Lewis quote comes from a segment on the ABC *7.30 Report* 30 July 2002. The transcript can be found at <www.abc.net.au/7.30/content/2002/s635781.htm>. The Humphries 'embarrassment' quote comes from the *Sunday Age*, 24 August 1997. Later quotes from Kennett come from the *Herald Sun*, 28 November 2011, and a personal interview conducted on 4 May 2012. The original designs for Federation Square are now held at the State Library of Victoria and are available online. The information on 'Nearamnew' comes from Paul Carter, *The making of Nearamnew at Federation Square*, MUP, Melbourne, 2005, and Emily Potter, 'New climate for an old world: Paul Carter's Nearamnew', *Artlink*, Vol. 29, No. 2, 2009. The Victorian Auditor-General's reports on Federation Square can be found at <download.audit.vic.gov.au/files/20020605-Executive-Summary-Public-Sector-Special_Review.pdf> and <http://download.audit.vic.gov.au/files/PSA_Report_May03.pdf>. Peter Seamer's views on the numbers at the open days comes from a personal interview, 29 March 2012. The Bracks speech and 'teacher' quote come from the *Sunday Age*, 27 October 2002.

CHAPTER THREE

The Civic and Cultural Charter can be found at <www.fedsquare.com>. Information on the Labyrinth comes from 'Federation Square – Design and Architecture' at <www.fedsquare.com>. Kate Brennan, Jane Sydenham-Clarke and Kimberley Polkinghorne were interviewed on 14 November 2011, 11 April 2012 and 15 June 2012.

CHAPTER FOUR

The Bernard Salt quote comes from the *Age*, 11 October 2003, while the recollection about the Iraq War demonstration from Bill Blakeney comes from a personal interview on 14 November 2011. My thanks to Tula Harris of Fed Square Pty Ltd for the statistics on visitor numbers and attitudes towards Federation Square. Information and reports on the 'Urban Screens' conference comes from Scott McQuire, Meredith Martin and Sabine Niederer (eds), *The Urban Screens Reader*, Institute of Network Cultures, Amsterdam, 2009 and an interview with Scott McQuire, Peter Chambers and Nikos Papastergiadis on 24 May 2012.

CHAPTER FIVE

On the car and suburbanisation in Melbourne see Graeme Davison, *Car Wars: How the Car Won Our Hearts and Conquered Our Cities*, Allen & Unwin, Sydney, 2004. On the decline of central cities in the United States in the postwar era see among others Witold Rybczynski, *City Life: Urban Expectations in a New World*, HarperCollins, Toronto, 1995, especially Ch. 5, 'The new downtown'. Ruth Glass coined the term 'gentrification' in *London: Aspects of Change*, MacGibbon & Kee, London, 1964. Jane Jacobs' most famous book was *The Death and Life of Great American Cities*, Random House, New York, 1961. The information on Millennium Park comes from Timothy J. Gilfoyle, *Millennium Park Chicago: Creating a Chicago Landmark*, Chicago University Press, 2006, while that on Paternoster Square and Liverpool One come from a *Guardian* series 'Privatising the outdoors: Who owns our public space', 11–13 June 2012. The Trafalgar Square information comes from <www.london.gov.uk/priorities/art-culture/trafalgar-square>. My thanks to Gilbert Rochcouste of 'Village Well' for his thoughts on these issues.

CONCLUSION

The recent criticism and defence of Federation Square was reported in the *Age* and *Herald Sun* on 3 and 4 April 2012. The Ethan Kent quote comes from a recent email to the Fed Square management team.

Photo: John Gollings